Creative
Catalyst

Creative Catalyst

Empowering
Experience Design Teams
From Ideation to Production

KILE OZIER

RIVERSHORE PRESS

To Joe, my father, from whom I believe I learned to dream.

When I was a boy, he flew his dream to heaven, leaving behind a little dreamer who continues to live inside of me.

To the thousands with dreams who did not live long enough to see them realized, some dying in the arms of loved ones, many dying alone.

And to Jaxon, who made me wait a long time, then showed up to love me...

...and to my continued amazement, still does!

CONTENTS

I'm a lucky man...
should one believe in luck.

I've lived my life, professional and personal, pretty much out on the proverbial limb, trusting my instincts, following my inspiration, and striving to do things the way I have thought right and best. Through this, a path of unique, personal experience has been walked; tests have been passed, obstacles overcome, and hundreds of thousands of audience members have left my stages and theatres carrying something special inside, to be remembered for a long time.

What I do know is that I am fortunate to have been born with a unique awareness of my surroundings, a sensitivity to those around me, and acute, naturally occurring powers of observation. My muse is observant and articulate, and I keep her nurtured and engaged as she participates in my life with me.

For years I did my thing—building spectacle, ceremony, and show, connecting with audiences—by the seat of my pants through instinct, until one day when a professional colleague asked me to speak to her group.

"What are your methodologies, and would you share them with us?"

Me: (blank stare)

I had absolutely no idea what my "methodologies" were. Truly, until that moment I'd never actually thought about a "process" and had been operating solely by instinct and logic.

So I first studied myself—deconstructing, examining, and defining my steps, methodologies, and techniques, which, though unnamed at the time, support me in delivering powerfully compelling, immersive, and experiential storytelling, messaging shows, and ceremonies. The physical metaphor that has always leapt to mind when I envision my own brain is a 3D chessboard with multiple simultaneous layers of play. That illustrates how I think. I see time almost physically in my mind, with shape and flow, and I can dynamically sort shifting priorities.

Next I analyzed and defined the steps in my creative and production processes, then backed into descriptions and names for them. I created my own terms that describe for me each of the steps that I embrace and use: my **Tenets for Creating Experience**. This was a great exercise, for deconstructing how I do it has made me even better at doing it.

This book, then, is intended to share from my own point of view what I hold as key tenets for the creation of experience and making emotional connection with audiences, whether that be a parade, show, or spectacle, a film or video, a ceremony or a speech. I will articulate, explain, and share those things that I consider to be integral to the creation of effective experience that is truly and resonantly immersive and emotionally connective—experience that compels response, and even action, from one's audiences.

Notice I do not say, **"THE Five Tenets of Experience Creation."** These are simply my tenets: tools, processes, steps, and practices at the core of pretty much everything I do. Applied to varying degrees and at different times, often several times at several junctures during the same project, they are the methodology through which I create.

1. Exploration of Assumption
2. Liberation from Preconception
3. Comfortable Disorientation
4. Successive Revelation
5. Subliminal Engagement

My intent is to make this information accessible and relevant as it applies across the board to creators, creatives, and those who manage and inspire them in a wide variety of industries. This book explores these philosophies and theories through practical examples and anecdotes from my body of work—some of which I'm proud, some of which I may be embarrassed, from all of which I have learned.

I trust you will find something here that will aid you in your particular endeavors.

Exploration Of Assumption

I n my experience, and probably in that of most all of us, assumption can be found at the root of virtually all misunderstanding. The insidious thing about assumption is that it is stealthy, pretty much ever-present, and most often goes completely unidentified and unrecognized. Thus, it calls for diligence.

It sounds and seems a simple and obvious maxim, yet the pervasiveness and profound effects can be easily missed until too late. As with the network of roots that thrive, interwoven beneath forest and meadow, with the propensity to sprout anywhere and at any time, assumption shows up everywhere. It can go unidentified while affecting nuance and substance or creative undertaking—holding us back from what is truly possible in the creation of something compelling.

It can be something as simple as the difference between the color "blue" as envisioned by a director when speaking of a set piece or lighting effect and the "blue" that is heard by the designer to whom they are speaking. And it can be the root cause of greater, deeper, and far more disparate differences. Undetected assumption can and will slow production, create unnecessary conflict between creatives, upset a producer (and we can't have that!), contribute to cost overruns, and—of the utmost importance—affect the resonance of the experience that is ultimately created and produced.

With all this at stake, **Exploration of Assumption** is therefore number one on my own list of **Tenets of Experience Creation**. Far from being a one-time practice or a moment in the course of development, this is, for me, a tool and practice appropriately and productively applied throughout any creative, collaborative process (and throughout life, for that matter).

Start by pondering a few questions:

1. What is the audience assuming when entering the theatre or space?
2. What am I assuming about that audience... and their assumptions, for that matter?
3. How might I be limiting myself and the spectrum of explorable possibility without realizing it?
4. What other subtle or blatant options, suggestions, or clues might be woven into the writing and reading of this script?
5. What might be outrageous...and how might that not be so outrageous?
6. What are the hidden possibilities inherent in a particular venue, theatre, or space?

Assumption is double-edged, sometimes there to be circumvented or overcome, while at other times an effective tool for leveraging and enhancing the experience. It isn't bad, as long as we recognize it. Unrecognized and unappreciated, assumption can undermine the process and the project. Awareness of it is always of value.

Throughout any process, from concept development through pre-production and production—even throughout the run of a show or experience—regularly pulling out the "What am I assuming" tool, examining the product or show, and examining my own ongoing decision-making has seldom failed to offer extra insights. Sometimes the smallest realization can be revelatory and can change the tone of what is being created.

Ask. Then listen.

Too often we see a significant missed step during the development process, costing millions of dollars, resulting in delays of months or even years, and causing no small amount of waste—resulting in a tragic shortfall of creative vision.

At a recent conference, a widely-respected leader of one of the more successful companies in the attractions design business was sharing anecdotes in the context of working in other cultures. The key point focused on the importance of listening when attempting to create, develop, work, and build in partnership with a foreign culture.

Two examples were provided wherein crucial, pertinent information came to light extremely late in the process. Had the principals not been listening with acuity at a fortunate, given moment, information critical to successful execution of the project might have been missed.

What I believe was actually missed was that the primary key to listening is asking questions early—questions that, in these instances, had not been asked.

Listening is of key importance. So often has a producer, director, or company parachuted into a foreign context and attempted to manifest some change or new thing without truly being in tune with the culture and specifics of the country or context. That being said, even the requisite listening must be guided by a preceding, underlying, fundamental discipline: asking. In sales and retail this has been called the open probe. The idea is to ask direct, focused questions that help those across the table explore their own assumptions about you, about themselves, and about their cultures and vision.

This chapter is about **Exploration of Assumption**, referring to the assumption(s) inherent in the vendor, audience, and visionary client. While working to realize the vision's full potential, both one's own assumptions as well as that of the client or audience may not be understood.

Assumption isn't always obvious. In fact, most often it is insidiously subtle. We assume things about our surroundings simply due to the fact that we see things a certain way through our own experiences, and thus tend to accept that this is the way these things are. And often, in the context of cultural idiosyncrasy, we don't even see for ourselves what we are assuming. If we don't see it, we can't alert others to it.

As the involved parties interact and exchange information, one must assiduously and regularly watch out for potential assumptions being made. It is easy to fail to do so, and such oversights will eat up time and resources in virtually every instance.

Right in front of your face

The first example from the presentation was of a theme park being built in Asia. Six months in, the site was locked and construction had begun, but the core theme—the overarching story that was to frame all the experiences in the park—had not yet been defined. Evidently the team had been exploring and pitching themes, but nothing had stuck.

One day when walking the property, someone on the local crew casually mentioned that the name of an adjacent mountain was "Phantom Mountain."

"What?!"

It turned out that a handy mystical legend that was eventually successfully developed into a compelling theme for the park had been sitting there, next to the property, the entire time. No one had thought to ask about adjacent topography.

Though presented as a delayed victory, I see this as a failed exploratory process. Months might have been saved had assumption been explored in the early meetings. Remember, it is not solely one's own assumptions that call for examination and circumventing; the client is also working through a personal filter of a set of unseen or unarticulated assumptions that they may not see as pertinent.

You gotta ask!

The client or host is immersed in an environment and culture that is as familiar as one's skin, leaving that person vulnerable to the inability to casually distinguish between what, to an outsider, may seem unique, and something that may be important to fuel or expedite a process. Thus, it takes extra discipline, and an acute focus on the part of the producer or creative director to dig for and elicit information that may not even seem important enough to mention.

Ask. Then listen.

The second anecdote was of an installation in an Arab country. With only a few days until opening it was announced that a special entrance to the property for the royals and VIPs had to be built. The usual Guest Services special entrance would not be sufficient for the culturally crucial special treatment of this upper of upper classes.

I can't imagine how this could have been missed in the very first meetings on design, not to mention the endless subsequent reviews and study over plans and schedules. Someone failed to ask a critical question, and an entire installation was designed and built without a crucial component.

This was not a failure to listen. It was a failure to ask—then listen.

Exploration of assumption is critical to every process and is not a one-time thing. One must keep in mind that we are very likely assuming most of the time, and so need to regularly apply the discipline of self-examination to avert an expensive, obstructive, and negative result. Concurrently, we must remember that those sitting across the table from us are also equally assuming deep and imperceptible wells of pertinent information that we, as concept developer, producer, or principal, need to know.

The opportunity to listen is around us at all times. Especially when parachuting into and moving through a new culture (any culture, actually, including one's own), keeping one's ears open at all times and hearing what's behind things that are said can result in the awareness and absorption of nuance that will very likely affect the creative process—and affect it positively when caught early.

An unexpected lesson

I often work in Dubai on various projects. One of the things I like so much about working in that part of the world is the mix of nationalities and cultures on pretty much any team of professionals one might encounter. It is not unusual to have team members who are English, Dutch, German, Indian, Pakistani, South African, American, and others. Together, in a culture alien to all of us, we work to deliver unsurpassable product to that client and in that culture. I appreciate my ability to be sensitive to the different cultures around me and keep the faux pas to a minimum, building and maintaining positive relationships with relative ease.

I say all this as a backdrop to a recent departure from the San Francisco airport when I was brought up short realizing I'd overlooked something very close to home. There is a gentleman at SFO whom I had not liked for years. He's always at the entry to the TSA queue and is a stickler for making sure the carry-on item fits into that ridiculous metal display that's supposed to determine whether or not it'll fit in the overhead compartment. Sometimes you can slip by him if the bag is carried deceptively or things are busy. But he will never allow a too-large bag to pass if he sees you.

I hadn't liked this guy since my first encounter with him years ago. When I interact with him I keep it congenial, swift, and professional, but inside I judged him a jerk. He's an older gentleman, east Asian, with a thickish accent that doesn't make it any easier to communicate when he's saying "no." Irascible and, in my opinion and experience, not the most pleasant person.

However…

I encountered him again during this latest trip. I was still out in the queue at the check-in counter, well before the security check. Then, just as I arrived at the ticket counter, up marched one of what I affectionately refer to as "The Entitled" (you may know the type—hotshot guys for whom No Rules Apply), dragging with him my you-shall-not-pass friend. Barging up to the agent standing next to me, he launched into a diatribe about this man's incompetence in his refusal to allow Mr. Entitled's truly massive rolling carry-on past the barrier.

Mr. Entitled was loud, brash, pushy, and especially disrespectful and dismissive of the man. He was berating him in the third person, never looking at or acknowledging him, while telling the agent about all the times he's had his bag on board with him—and "who does this guy think he is," telling him any different.

I didn't feel like watching, so I moved on to the security area and—about four minutes later—the gentleman walked past the queue to his regular place at the head of the rope and stanchion, the physical entry to the TSA queue. Slowly, he bent over, picked up his gloves, and then stared out at…I don't know what he saw, actually. He stared in the direction of those of us waiting in the queue, but sort of through us, over our heads or beyond where we were standing.

And in that moment, what I saw broke my heart. What I now saw was a man from another culture, deeply dedicated to his job. Dedicated to…and proud of it. Suddenly, I re-appreciated his own, inherent, cultural roots; he comes from a culture where rules aren't mere rules, where rules and order are respected…and they do apply. I saw that all he was doing—all he had ever been doing—had been ensuring that the rules were followed.

He had simply been doing a job he was grateful to have and proud to do. I saw him hurt and perhaps shamed to have had his competence questioned. I have no idea the outcome of the altercation at the ticket counter; all I saw was the starkly visual, personal result of the insult. The wound I perceived in his eyes made me ashamed of all the times I had thought ill of him. He looked around the airport, turned, picked up his jacket and put it under his arm. Head down, he left the area.

I realized in that moment that I'd short-circuited one of my most valued personal and professional qualities by assuming and compartmentalizing. Empathy, cross-cultural, and inter-cultural sensitivity are of my best qualities. I'm good at making my way in alien cultures, appreciating my own sensitivities that serve me well in my work, especially in Dubai and places similar to it.

When in Dubai, though, it's easy to remember to remain culturally sensitive, as one is constantly surrounded with reminders of one's own foreignness through accents, clothing, skin color, and mannerisms. It was right there, at home of all places, where I'd overlooked the very clues I seek to recognize when I'm aware. I'd missed a crucial opportunity to exemplify behaviors I embrace when traveling.

We should always strive to be aware. And beware the pitfalls of familiarity that lead to any assumptions, erroneous or otherwise. Exploration of Assumption is the first tenet of my Big Five for the creation of compelling experience. Exploring, or being aware of, one's own assumptions is a valuable tool in all situations—not just the important ones.

Here's the lesson for all of us, including myself

Practice at home what we practice in the field. Assume nothing and watch for one's own assumptions in every aspect of daily life, in both personal and professional interactions. Be and remain sensitive to others and guard against judgment on the basis of anything from facial expression to uniform.

I now believe that my airport friend has never sought to be unpleasant or difficult; he doesn't even see it that way. He has simply been striving to do his job the best way he understands that it needs to be done. It's not up to me to judge him, nor to like or dislike his style. Rather, I'm offered the opportunity to simply accept that it is what it is. The man's been there for years; someone must appreciate and approve of the way he does his job.

People around us, throughout our personal and professional lives, all have backstories and histories of which we know nothing. So much that we might tend to take personally, or take onboard in frustration, might very easily spring from reasonable sources or rationale outside our own experience—from things we do not know. My suggestion is to accept it and move on in situations such as this one. In our ongoing professional lives, then, when someone isn't responding as we might prefer, perhaps it's a healthy modus operandi to call to mind such lessons and just work with what we have.

Don't assume—ask

Whenever I'm preparing for a period of work immersion in a culture completely foreign to me, I take care through the preceding days to carefully examine my emotional baggage cart for that insidious passenger—assumption.

It's everywhere.

In the run-up to any given project, where I will be working through interpreters in multiple contexts, my awareness of assumption in daily social and professional intercourse becomes heightened even further, such that I begin to recognize its pervasiveness in everything from dinner conversations to elevator chat.

Listen.

The key to being aware of the presence of assumption—one's own and that of colleagues, clients, and others—is to listen. Listening acutely to everyone at the table, hearing what is said and extrapolating what may actually lie behind it...all the while remaining conscious of its ramifications to the course of conversation and the quality of decisions being made.

There's a reason we'll continue dwelling on this concept. It's because assumption is The One Thing, passively dismissed, that runs rampant and unidentified through most conversations between human beings of every culture. It causes subtle misunderstandings that can build upon one another and steer processes off track without people even noticing.

It is easiest to detect assumption in what isn't said just before what is said. To discern that, one's listening must be focused on the conversation rather than figuring out what one is about to say next. Almost everything that comes out of our mouths is based on some sort of assumption we make just prior to speaking. It may be about a creative process, an approach to the resolution of a previously-encountered problem, or even the personal resonance of a "shared" experience.

What do I mean by that? Few professionals would tell themselves that their methods are "the only way" to accomplish a given task or project. That being said, many a time I've watched as misunderstandings evolved through the use of "common" terms in conversations referencing disparate experiences. I've watched conversations go off-track as underlying misunderstandings roll along unidentified while people think they are making themselves clear, when the opposite may actually be the case.

A good rule of thumb when listening is to ask yourself if you fully comprehend what is being said...or is assumption already at play? If so, clear it up. Now.

The open probe

Challenging someone directly with, "...well, you're assuming..." or "...aren't you assuming..." isn't the most productive nor effectively diplomatic way to address and derail assumption. Instead, try the open probe approach; it can open a doorway to heightened understanding in a matter of moments.

What might this look like?

"Could you say more about that?"

"Actually, that's not clear to me; would you expand on that...?"

"You know what, I'm not quite getting this...Could you give me an example of what you are talking about? I just want to be sure I get it."

Contrary to what one might assume, this does not protract the process. While it may slow the meeting, as clarifications are made and appreciation of common-ground communication is uncovered, it will probably shorten the overall process and possibly lower the overall project cost.

Meanwhile, it is wise to be aware that a question can come across as a challenge, and to choose language that does not fuel that perception. If one comes from a place of truly wishing to comprehend and appreciate, and is confident in that desire to know in order to move things forward and facilitate understanding, chances are that motive will communicate itself in tone and word.

Ask questions—don't assume knowledge.

Listen for assumptions of others and be sure that what is really meant is actually understood...by you, by everyone. With careful attention to assumption, success is more certain.

Creative Catalyst

2

Liberation From Preconception

Crossing the very fine—though deeply nuanced—line that lies between the minefield of unexplored assumption and preconception is where one often encounters the product of those pesky assumptions that call for exploration throughout the process of creative development and production. Preconception springs eternal, from the mounting of a production in a venue, theatre, or location with which an audience is already familiar, to telling a story the audience is inclined to think they already know. People think they know all the stories and how each is told.

Let 'em think that...until they are in your control, under your influence. Then turn the proverbial tables. Sometimes this can be as simple as rotating a room and entering through an unforeseen doorway, entering a theatre through the stage door and across the stage, or even seating the audience on the stage while the performance comes from other parts of the auditorium. You've probably done this sort of thing in your work, installations, and productions.

The thing about preconception is that it's a conversation going on inside the head of an audience member, reassuring them that they are, indeed, on top of this thing. They know what's going to happen, what happens after that, and then what's after that. Within seconds after an experience has launched each individual can be rapt in their own, individual reveries, cued by what's onstage. But they may not be immersed in the story you're attempting to tell.

On the one hand, this is great; the audience is happy, as they are getting what they expected. They expected to like it and they do. Nice. Nice emotions come to the fore;

nice memories come off the virtual shelf. The experience is nice. I think, though, that we can often dig far deeper into the store of cherished experience when striving to evoke and connect than is most commonly executed.

Stanford University Campaign

Here's an example to illustrate this idea. In creating the opening film for a national tour of campaign experience for Stanford University Alumni, I strove to create something that would re-ignite the wonder and excitement of discovering that campus for the first time. Up to then, pretty much every media piece for the university traditionally opened with a shot of the iconic, main entrance to the campus—Palm Drive, along with the Oval, the Arches, the Quad, Memorial Church, the foothills in the background, or some combination of these. The same approach was reflected in most major print pieces of the institution.

My theory is that when presented with such a regular and familiar (though beautiful) litany of imagery, the minds and imaginations of the audience are immediately stimulated to call up the easiest memories— games of frisbee on the oval lawn, who they played with, what a great time the university years were. Within seconds they've left the experience and narrative that's unfolding before them and are instead off on their own familiar path of reverie. Again, nice, though perhaps not as deeply moving and compelling as it might be.

So, what we designed was a short, wordless film backed by a lush, evocative score that began with a solo cyclist in the foothills behind campus. These foothills are protected land, and any experience an alum would have of these would be an intimate one: a lone exploratory walk, a small practical seminar, time with a loved one, even a proposal of marriage...no large groups or big experiences. This set the stage from the outset for circumventing and liberating preconception.

The journey of three minutes brought our cyclist out of the foothills and onto campus from the back side, taking a bit of a circuitous route past familiar architecture and landmarks, along the lake, past the stables, down fraternity row, through this plaza and that archway, with familiar campus activities taking place as he passed by. The net effect was a tour of campus with quick glimpses of the new, adjacent to the familiar.

Suddenly the clock began to strike and the cyclist realized he was going to be late for class. Speeding up as he flew past students and classrooms, he arrived at his destination at the final second, just as his professor (familiar to generations of alumni) entered and the seminar began.

As he breathed a sigh of relief the camera left him and, as the music built, a rapid montage of photos from eleven decades of university history flew past to reveal a panoramic flyover shot of what the audience had expected to see at the beginning of the film—the oval, the church,

the quad, and the arches. Not a single soul there was disappointed; most all were able to see these icons in a different light than had they been presented as matter-of-fact at the beginning.

During the first thirty seconds of the film the audience went completely quiet, save the occasional gasp of recognition of a building or pathway. At the end of the three minutes, however, the audience erupted into spontaneous applause and cheering to match that of the film's soundtrack. Their heads and hearts were indisputably back "on campus," and they were freshly aware of an excitement rarely felt since adolescence. They also realized they didn't know what was coming next; anticipation was heightened in the room.

It worked. You can watch the film, and others mentioned in this book, on my YouTube channel.

Harvard Law School

Applying this same theory, it worked in a very different way when launching a development campaign at Harvard Law School.

It's a fairly safe assumption that the law library is the core of the law school experience—the heart, the fulcrum. (This remains an assumption, of course; site-specific research is always in order.) In their first days on campus new students enter this august and historic space—this hallowed hall—with anticipatory, aspirational reverence, bated breath, and wide eyes. The entrance to this vast, rectangular space is in the middle of the long side of the room. Stepping into the central atrium, the eyes are drawn to the facing bank of floor-to-ceiling windows that look out onto Holmes Field. But then, once one reaches the center, the immensity of the colonnade of books that reach left and right and stretch to the distant ends of the hall communicate, materially, the amount of knowledge that awaits.

The romance and magic of that first moment dissipates over the first months as the law library comes to represent hundreds of hours of brain-straining study on the path toward degree. We wanted to gift the returning alumni with a new experience of the space, one that might restore the breathtaking beauty and re-instill the reverence for the immersive architectural experience.

We did not bring the audience into the library for the main event the way they'd always entered this space. During their time in school the place had transformed from awe and inspiration into a dreaded, hated destination. Rather than invoke memories of arduous toil,

Creative Catalyst

we devised a way to present the space to them from a perspective that most, if not all, had never before actually experienced. From the lawn outside, we routed them up three flights of emergency stairs, through the emergency exit at the point furthest from the atrium, into the stacks of the darkly-lit library. Each alum's first look at the room was of a beautiful garden of knowledge.

The entire space, featuring the Roman columns, was lit to enhance the architecture, as boxwood trees and tiny lights accented the beauty of the room itself as well as what it contains. Gasps of awe and appreciation were welcome evidence of success in giving our guests a vision they'd not before experienced, reigniting the wonder of the place in their own memories. They entered and saw the beauty of the unobstructed rows of columns bisecting the room and the never-ending book stacks, viewed from the long perspective they never witnessed.

Suddenly, these jaded lawyers were immersed in the beauty of the library and reminded of the reverence with which they had once held these thousands of tomes. We circumvented all expectation, liberated them from self-taught preconception, and, by taking them to a room they thought they knew fully, comfortably disoriented them in the gentlest, most evocative way.

Sly. Effective. Gentle. Moving to experience.

3

**Comfortable
Disorientation**

At the core of my **Five Tenets** is this one, which would be my favorite if I had to pick just one. It's also probably the most important on the list. Though, as with anything woven or interrelated, all of these depend on the presence and exercise of the other four in order to be fully effective.

Comfortable disorientation pretty much articulates what I believe underlies the success achieved when the spectrum of these tenets are applied to best effect. It's when the audience members or guests temporarily forget everything outside the experience and find themselves fully immersed and given over to your control, feeling safe in not knowing what's next...

And that's the key— feeling safe in not knowing what's next.

To create in one fell swoop, both a sense of disorientation as well as the sense of being safe and taken care of, finding comfort in the unexpected. To virtually pull the rug from beneath them while assuring them of the presence of a safety net. Effectively executed, this technique results in an immediate deeper level of trust on the part of the audience and an intangible, yet greater, willingness to suspend disbelief. To further quiet the left brain and allow us to wrangle their right lobes, taking them further into fantasy and reverie.

Once they know that they don't know, and realize that they're "safe"—the guests become more completely ours for the journey we host. Camaraderie comes from the fact that each individual is experiencing the instant dissolution of preconception and the concomitant reassurance that something possibly better and certainly more interesting may await. Yet all are sharing this unique yin–yang at precisely the same moment, in the same time and place. This creates an instant, deep connection amongst the audience, as no longer is the experience simply a shared one; it is unique and happening only here, only now.

Theme parks strive for this all the time, often with what I call the **Venice Effect**. Guests are brought through a queue that is often labyrinthine, usually feeling a bit cramped with limited sight-lines and low ceilings, to then be suddenly released into a space that seems vast by comparison.

Creators of experience virtually always have disorientation or comfort in play in any created or produced experience or show. It is the presence of both, in the right balance and with the right timing, that has the inherent power to render an experience most deeply compelling and resonant. This might be accomplished through a move so simple as that of bringing an audience into a theatre or venue via backstage, perhaps starting in an alley with no hint at the ultimate destination space. Preconception is avoided entirely (we've liberated them from that!). They're backstage before they realize it's an actual backstage; it's at the moment they walk across the stage and into the auditorium that they actually appreciate where they are. They then have the opportunity to see the auditorium or space, of which they may have a previous experience, from an entirely different perspective.

Disorientation. Comfort.

Stanford University Theatrical Tour

One of the most effective instances where I applied this idea was for a theatrical tour for Stanford University. It was simple, powerful, low-tech, and inexpensive. The day began with a typical conference and cocktail reception. Nothing new there. But then it was time for dinner. The gong sounded, the doors flew open, and the guests began to pour into what they thought was the "ballroom." But...no...

A vast, high-ceilinged, unlit space lay before them. Some thirty yards distant across the dark floor was a free-standing, 20-foot circular curtain curving left and right away from them; from over the top spilled a bright, warm light. Their destination was clear: this "island" of light floating in the darkness—a safe place. In the darkness between doorway and destination, volunteers stood in rows on either side of the pathway, shining flashlights across the floor to verify there were no cables, trapdoors, or obstacles to trip guests on their way toward the sparkling destination across the space.

Palette of preconception thusly cleared and audience effectively disoriented, they were at the same time reassured that this had been carefully planned. There was no doubt where they were headed and how they were going to get there...intrigue and excitement built, as they still did not know what was behind the curtain.

Once across the space and having passed through the curtained barrier, the guests entered a space-within-a-space to find themselves surrounded with architectural iconography from every decade of the University's history. Familiar landmarks from across campus, in various

Creative Catalyst

sizes and scales, were represented in two and three dimensions as well as by projection. Immersed in the colors, textures, and visual cues from their own experiences on campus, as they looked closer each could see that these icons were juxtaposed with one another in unusual ways, quite dissimilar from their geographical relationships on campus.

This mixture of differing scales, formats, and dimension, along with familiar colors and shapes, combined to fuel curiosity and intrigue. It compelled them to look closer, to explore and become familiar with what had been previously familiar in their past; to rediscover those iconic buildings and installations of which they had had previous experience.

The result leaves them disoriented, and quite comfortably so.

This approach can be applied to a variety of experience types. The one for Stanford was an event, but one can use similar techniques for nearly anything, including theatrical shows, pop-up marketing, theme parks—anything that involves an experience. It's different every time and for every client or story to be told; it takes application of the previous two tenets to get to the point of discovering how to comfortably disorient. In my experience, it's well worth the work.

Surprise sans startle.

Awe without shock.

Comfortable disorientation.

4

Successive Revelation

Don't give it all away at once. Similar to the nurturing of a relationship, one doesn't want to pour it all out on the first date and risk overwhelming the person. Too much up front can completely overload the audience early on and numb them to further sensation, empathy, or inspiration; this can leave them inured to subtlety and nuance as the story or experience unfolds. They depart "blown away" perhaps, though possibly not moved as deeply or as compellingly as they might otherwise be had a lighter hand been used.

Instead, I try to shape the arc of storytelling such that I can share a little, create some curiosity, share a little bit more, pay off a bit of curiosity, and with each successive revelation ramp up the level of intimacy—the depth of the experience. With this tool I make my audiences more and more comfortable, gradually letting down their guard and giving themselves over to the experience through which I plan to lead them. Sort of like cooking a lobster, I suppose—that virtual water gradually warms up, guests' defenses dissolve, and their emotions become mine to "devour" by manipulation.

In the Stanford University film project we discussed in chapter two, this dynamic was accomplished obliquely, revealing the modern campus bit by bit as the cyclist rode past traditional icons as well as newer additions... giving the audience brief moment after moment of vision, discovery, recognition, and exhilaration. A well-crafted experience can unfold through a number of such experiences—each created to reveal a piece of story, the answer to a previously-posed question, the solution to a practical riddle or dilemma. All of it builds on what has come before, as the journey from curtain-up to curtain call continues.

Creative Catalyst

I used to call this gasp and grasp, drawn from the simultaneous occurrence of the physical intake of breath as people recognize or appreciate the tidbit being revealed, compelling a subsequent, virtual "reaching-out" for the next morsel of story. Effective use of this technique engages the audience and creates a dynamic whereby they are in a subtle, constant cycle of anticipation and reward—primed for maximum appreciation should there be an emotional or celebratory final moment.

In my seminars, I share this slide:

"THAT WAS AMAZING!"

"That...was amazing!"

Each instance is set in a different font. I then ask if anyone can differentiate between the two statements. The first one is what most big experiences deliver, spoken as a teenager might exclaim after a rollercoaster ride, "That was AWESOME, dude!" This version is what most good storytellers deliver to their audiences.

But what I strive for is better represented by the second "That...was amazing!" This one, spoken in a gentle, thoughtful, and almost reverential whisper, reflects the individual having experienced something profound in a way that may be too subtle to even articulate, though it remains with the audience member long after the house has gone dark and the audience departed. What I seek is to create experience that awaits my guests upon awakening the following morning, for images and feelings to continue to wash and swirl within them as they kiss their partners good morning and share a bit about what they experienced the evening before.

Don't give it all away at once.

The Venice Effect

I spent my college sophomore year in Pavia, Italy, a quiet-ish town just twenty miles south of Milano. Possessed of the requisite number of churches, a cathedral, a central town square, covered bridge over the Ticino River, and stone-paved streets, for me Pavia was the perfect combination of town and village to host a first-time expatriate experience. The University of Pavia, one of the oldest universities in the world (pre–825AD), boasts an impressive list of alumni that includes Christopher Columbus, Camillo Golgi, Antonio Scarpa, multiple Nobel Prize winners, and famous names from philosophy, law, and medicine—none of whom are related to me.

Effectively my first fully-immersive experience, I lived in Collegio Fraccaro, one of two Americans amongst two hundred medical students—few of whom spoke English. This alone helped transform the learning of Italian from an academic exercise into a survival tool. It was a wonderful year and has remained vivid in my memory ever since. I swam with and helped coach the city swim team, hitchhiked all over Northern Italy, Switzerland, and

Austria on weekends, went to the annual Sagra (Festival) in scores of nearby local towns and villages as each celebrated their Thing of Most Pride (usually edible—no problem), and spent time with hundreds of locals as I became more proficient in the language.

Through the winter I had dinner twice a month with a local businessman and his family. We'd met through the proprietress of my favorite café; I suppose she was my "dealer," so to speak, as that was the birthplace of my lifelong addiction to espresso and strong coffee. The rule at these dinners was that I was to speak only Italian while he would only speak English, except for instances when we needed to correct each other. This was for him and his wife the opportunity to give their kids a head start on learning English; it certainly benefited me as well. The food was great, and conversations would inevitably wax more complex as the evening progressed and the level of proficiency increased.

But one such night stands out among them all: the night in February when I mentioned that in a few weeks I was going to see Venice for the first time.

"Ahh, Venezia!" he sang. *"Il cuore d'Italia!"* (The heart of Italy)

And with that, the English lesson was over as his passion took flight...

Passionately, his hands conducting an unseen orchestra, he began instructing me on how to approach and see Venice for the first time.

"Senti!" (Listen!)

"Quando arrivi a Venezia, non vai subito a Piazza San Marco!"
(Do not go immediately to Piazza San Marco!)

"No. Stay away from Venice proper 'til early morning. Then, before the sun rises, take the *vaporetto* (waterbus) to the far side of the island—NOT to Piazza San Marco.

"Walk the *vicoli* (alleyways)...*perditi come tu vaghi* (lose yourself as you wander)...*ascoltare alla città* (listen to the city)...

"Wander...

"Keep wandering. See the city awaken. Observe. Immerse." (I don't know that he actually said "immerse," but that was the concept). "You will forget where you are...and then..."

(Dramatic pause. He looked me directly in the eye.)

"Suddenly...you will discover Piazza San Marco!

"And then...you will understand Venezia...and then...you will understand Italia..."

...and he rested his hands on his stomach as he leaned back against his chair.

So that's what I did.

Arriving late the night before, I was just in time to check into the youth hostel on the island of Giudecca, coincidentally almost directly across the water from Piazza San Marco. I could see the towers and dome of the Basilica from my room, but the lower levels were obscured by buildings.

Creative Catalyst

In the dark of the next morning, refusing to look across the water, I boarded the *vaporetto*, traveled to the far side of the Castello district, alighted at Ospedale, and began to wander. By now the sky was grey and I could hear activity behind the windows I passed. Venturing just a few steps from the ocean, I found myself in the narrowest of passageways without view of any sort of landmark, as the vicoli can be as narrow as three feet with walls several stories high. There is virtually no way to know where one is in relation to anything else. Fortunately, there is water in all directions, so at some point one will inevitably arrive at an edge...and water. Thus, onward!

Narrow bridges over cramped canals are barely wider than a gondola; gondoliers call to one another as they wipe down their barche and begin navigating toward the Grand Canal and the morning fares. Passageways are just wide enough for people with small carts—every inch of Venice is valuable and there is no wasted space. I could hear the *chiacchierare* of morning television, the clang of pots on stoves, clatter of dishes on tables, and mothers calling for the *ragazzi* to get themselves down to breakfast. In tiny interior plazas fishermen were piling high their fresh catches onto tabletops, hosing down the pavestones to be ready to sell lunch and dinner to the shopping mothers once their kids have left for school. Up high, the sky is blue, though one only sees a sliver... even passing through the morning marketplaces, the view is still high above. One can only see what's adjacent—nothing distant, no landmarks.

But that limitation went completely unrealized, as I was immersed in the activity and detail all around me...and navigating through it. Objectively, I knew I was heading in the general direction of Piazza San Marco, though I really wasn't thinking about it with so much going on around me.

I came upon a fountain...

The base was carved with little bowls into which slender streams of water were fed as part of the runoff. At that moment one of them was functioning as a birdbath, wherein a couple of *piccioni* were taking their morning ablutions. I leaned in to get a photograph (with an actual Nikon camera—that's how long ago this was), and as I stood up and looked across the fountain...

There it was! Piazza San Marco.

It was breathtaking—the vastness of the Piazza was magnificent. The effect of encountering so much unencumbered space, being able to see the sunshine sparkling on the waterway to the left, warming the rooftops above the surrounding colonnade and shining bright on buildings far away...brightening the white stones of the plaza to alabaster, then turning and seeing the brilliant façade of the Basilica...

It stopped me completely. I don't know that I'd ever before been moved by architecture, but my eyes were wet and my throat hurt as I immediately appreciated the investment in the ethereal that had been made in the creation of this space. Had I gone directly to the Piazza, I know I would still have been impressed. It is beautiful. It's really not so big; as piazze go, it's not spectacular. In its Venetian context, though, it is virtually unsurpassed in grandeur, in eloquence, in transcendence.

I don't know that I understand Italy, or Venice, but I certainly discovered and embraced something I felt at

Creative Catalyst

that moment that can only be appreciated by walking through it. It is a moment and an experience I shall never forget: March of 1972.

It wasn't until years later that I realized the opportunity to use that morning in Italia to enhance audience experience. Introducing an audience into a space, even and often more effectively into a space with which they are presumptively familiar, through a distracting, engaging, and perhaps somewhat confining pathway has never failed to engage even the most jaded at some subliminal level. I call it the **Venice Effect**.

Offering people a new perspective on familiar things is an unexpected gift that can affect how we might experience other things to which we may have become familiar. The opportunity is there to see through fresh lenses, remove preconception, and make the old new. I wonder if we might be able to find a way, within each of ourselves, to do this with other people—to refresh our vision and brush away years of familiarity to see how those around whom we have spent so much time may have grown or evolved since we first met. To hold close the love and fondness that may have grown between friends and colleagues over the years, while seeing the new person right before our eyes—and to be seen, each of us, for who we have become as we've been so busy being.

There is no app for that.

5

**Subliminal
Engagement**

nvite the audience to participate in the creation of their own experience. Well executed, constructing an experience that subliminally engages participants can make for an intimate and very personal experience for each individual, irrespective of theatre or audience size.

Another way to put it is to "give the audience some of the work." Create an experience that is in some ways incomplete, leaving it to each audience member to "complete" for oneself. The set, a song, a word or conclusion...rather than hand it all to them, rather than fully articulating each thing in any dimension, provide hints. Lead them to something but don't take them all the way. Allow for the journey to be completed in the imaginations of the audience members.

With finesse, something almost magical can happen. You can offer each person in the audience the discovery or rediscovery of something intensely personal. What ramps up the resonance, the intensity of the experience, is that most every participant can experience this personal epiphany at virtually the exact same moment. This offers a theatre-wide, palpable, almost physical rush that renders the experience exponentially more powerful.

Evocation versus articulation

The most universally-recognized example of this would likely be Julie Taymor's costume designs for *The Lion King*. These costumes evoke jungle animals rather than attempt to fully articulate them. What happens in the mind of each audience member is the recognition of a hyena, a zebra, or a gazelle.

Not just any hyena or zebra is perceived, however, and not the same one by all in the theatre. Rather, each person recognizes a specific, individual personal experience of "zebra"—the animal that they know or may have experienced. Yet it is a shared personal experience, the power of which cannot be overstated despite the virtual nature of it. This experience is borne of subliminal engagement.

Back to the Stanford project from chapter two, this was the primary goal of creating a film that was shot with two adjacent cameras and projected on two adjacent screens separated by about fifteen feet of stage.

The separation of the screens was key to the vitality of the experience.

When watched in situ, the imaginations of the audience subconsciously pulled those screens together, creating the single perceived image; they were working to create their own experience side-by-side with one another. There is a sublime exultation that effervesces within each of us as we watch, engage, and create the very experiences that we are appreciating and enjoying. In a sense, we are discovering.

> The Stanford films, primarily "Back to the Farm" and "Symphony of Voices," can be seen on my YouTube channel.

An extreme example of this is darkness—a traditional theatrical technique—punctuated with light for the action, sounds and effects broadcast into darkness, bare stages with boxes, ladders, and spartan sets. While that can work, care must be exercised in the avoidance of going too far in one direction, risking boredom or distraction by the very spareness that is meant to do the evoking.

I believe what gives this its power and effectiveness is the lushness or completeness of what is articulated, rendering what is missing that much more dissonant— and by that dissonance, that absence, calling forth more colorful and complete imagery and experience from the imagination.

There are myriad ways of creating experience that elicit subliminal engagement: observe, examine, invent, adopt...create.

Underproduction by design

Restraint

Restrained by budget

Restrained by time

Restrained by resource

Restrained by design

This isn't specifically one of my Tenets, but simply a feature of the process—most of the time.

I'll wager that we all encounter the first three of these regularly. Budgets, floor space, ceiling height, and so on are almost always smaller than the vision of the client or creative who wants a brilliant and fully fleshed-out concept squeezed immediately from some toothpaste tube of creativity. These constraints are the obstacles that challenge us to stretch our creative muscle, finding ways to surmount and ensure quality of the experience we are creating for our audiences.

Interestingly, more times than not it seems these challenges tend to result in a process that enhances the experience. I view this constraint as another form of discipline as we navigate the channels of creativity and production. It also keeps things interesting.

Sometimes, though, by taking subliminal engagement to a virtual extreme one can achieve a powerfully compelling result through spare production by design. Underproduction, while maintaining finesse and elegance, can actually captivate and engage an audience. Less is indeed significantly—if not substantially—more.

Effectively realized, a huge open dark space far larger than the audience it is meant to contain can become an immersive theatre, an experiential time machine of sorts. Lit with "islands" of light as performance spaces with a combination of physical expanse and visual darkness, where participants cannot even see the distant enclosing walls, this minimalist staging can support a fuller suspension of disbelief. The audience is comfortably disoriented and the experience is successively revealed as sounds come out of the darkness, lights fade in to spotlight a moment of action or narrative, then fade out. Individuals are left subliminally engaged as each person weaves the connective thread of their own making through the experience(s) offered them.

Obviously, sight lines and acoustics must support the experience, and more than some cinder blocks and flashlights are necessary to render the ignition of imagination. That being said, much can be accomplished—much experience communicated—by evoking with sound, revealing bits and pieces with light.

Candlelight and fireworks

I am lucky to have been able to see two similar experiences created at the same venue, years apart and with essentially the same program format, and to witness the difference in audience response to the different approaches. Full disclosure: I produced and directed the event that I found most effective and compelling. I believe, though, that I am being objective in my assessment, but if not, well, there it is.

When asked which of my own productions I am most proud of, one of the top three is the Candlelight Ceremony for the AIDS Memorial Quilt at the Lincoln Memorial in 1992. Twenty years later, this still ranks as one of my finest accomplishments and, in retrospect, all of my tenets were applied to its creation. Of course, at the time I had not given terms or definitions to my methodologies—it was all instinct.

Using what was there, we designed our lighting towers and screens such that views of the reflecting pool, the steps leading to the Memorial, and the Memorial itself remained unobstructed. The Memorial was our stage, and my sense was that to augment it would be to distract. So, no stage was built; all support, backstage, and green room facilities were completely out of view, and the Memorial was lit only from towers hidden in the trees.

Well, that...and the glow from the candles held in the darkness by the 250,000 gathered marchers.

The program consisted of an august roster of speakers and performers who were famous at the time: singer Patti Austin, Representative Eleanor Holmes Norton, Cleve Jones (founder of the National AIDS Memorial Quilt), actress and performer Liza Minnelli (as speaker rather than performer—liberation of preconception!— she offered the spiritual moment...an effectively unexpected use of preeminent talent), with Academy Award Winner Joel Grey singing the finale.

The program went up at 8pm and was to close at 8:45. There was no flexibility in this schedule, as Representative Nancy Pelosi had arranged for a 5-minute window of no air traffic over the Potomac for my final effect (hang on, I'll tell you...). So that was that— no one was allowed to run past their scheduled times (we'll cover techniques for that a bit later).

Going into this project, I had developed a reputation for doing fireworks, indoors, at many of my ceremonies and productions in and around San Francisco. The casual joke among my friends and those who were familiar with my work was, "How are you going to write fireworks into this one, Kile?" If anything, this came closest to a memorial service, and there was no appropriate place for celebratory fireworks. There was nothing to celebrate; hundreds of thousands of our friends had died and were still dying as the scourge of AIDS took them from us.

The final piece, though, was Mr. Grey singing "Jonathan Wesley Oliver, Jr.," a song sung by a man who has come to the Quilt to say goodbye to his boyhood buddy, of whom "somebody told me you would be here..." If you are not familiar with it, this is a very poignant and sad song, one of loss and forgiveness, redemption, and nostalgia for an innocent time. The song speaks of when the two were kids, just farm boys playing in the fields and sitting on bales of hay at night, talking and looking for shooting stars. The final line in the song is,

"Tell me, Jonathan, up in Heaven, are there shooting stars...?"

The great pyrotechnician George Zambelli had built for me a single, giant, bright-white skyrocket that would explode silently...sparkling brilliance and absolute silence. As Joel Grey held his last note, the audience could see the tail of the rocket weaving upwards from behind the Memorial, then fill the sky with shimmering brilliance.

And at that moment, all one could hear was the simultaneous, spontaneous, quietly personal gasp as the breath of each of the 250,000 people caught in their throats.

Overproduction

"The Left Brain and What's Right"
or
The Perils of TMI (Too Much Information)

Tell 'em everything, show 'em everything, lay it all out and your audience will leave with less than you might otherwise have given them had the experience been better crafted to engage. Don't just spell it out for them; less truly is more, more often than not, and to articulate every moment, point, and beat of a story does a disservice to our audience.

In conversations with clients it is not unusual to hear arguments in favor of spelling things out "in case someone doesn't get it." Well, we can certainly do that, but giving it all away makes it a show, whereas offering a well-crafted, creative "less" can elevate that show

into an experience that is deeper and more resonant—
and more personal. As we've discussed earlier, let the
audience do some of the work.

It seems many producers and directors strive to erad-
icate any doubt in the minds of an audience as to what
is intended or meant, the thoughts of the main char-
acters, the why that motivates each action or word.
Leading the audience step-by-step through a story may
seem thorough and complete in theory. And, in a sense,
it is both thorough and complete, but such completeness isn't necessarily a foundation for powerful storytelling. Sometimes, allowing the audience to draw their
own conclusions based on their experience of what you
have presented can result in deeply-felt convictions as
to motive and eventuality—and it will differ widely from
seat to seat in your theatre.

Our earlier discussion of subliminal engagement and
the liberation of preconception reinforces this idea
that filling in all the blanks and wrapping everything in
a no-loose-ends bow isn't necessarily the most effective approach. There are also theories and methodologies of communication with an audience through the
left and right lobes of the brain that apply. This division
of cerebral labor is, I think, often discussed or refer-
enced, yet not so often actually examined and applied
in the context of creating event or ride experience,
producing theatre, or even making film and video for
the occasional capital campaign.

As you likely know, the left brain leans toward the
analytical while the right largely manages feelings
and emotions—the cerebral versus the visceral. That
being the case, there are some general rules I tend to

follow as much as possible when creating film, video, or theatre in order to keep the left brain quiet (if not dormant) and the right brain engaged and active.

On-screen text

When creating film, the banning of print or titles from the screen is worthy of exploration and adherence. A line must often be walked, especially when on-camera interviews are a part of the piece, with deciding how and when to identify a given speaker. If you can get away without identifying a person, then by all means do it!

Depending on your audience and familiarity with the speaker, identification may not even be necessary. Perhaps you could list them at the beginning or end of the video. Write the script so that each person references who's coming up next. Maybe try a light-handed use of narration between segments. Find a way that's best for your storytelling without obstruction; there isn't always a way, but there very often is at least one.

Data & information

Frankly, there is rarely a situation where it serves the delivery of information to put data on-screen. More often than not that data can "date" a video almost overnight. One can refer to data, fact, and figure, leaving it to the audience to dig further as desired.

We did this for a non-profit capital campaign in southern California a few years back with actress Jane Seymour as our star and ambassador. She described the experience, engaging the audience with her description of the programs, but only making reference to the innumerable details. "Don't worry," she says to the camera, "I'm not going to show you all those facts and figures; that's why we have Google!" Worked like a charm.

Some years back a famous event designer from a major eastern city created some fantastic centerpieces composed entirely of red and yellow roses. He took apart one color of rose and, petal by petal, tucked those alternate colors into the contrasting bloom. It was very impressive, clearly an intricate, laborious, and expensive augmentation of the evening.

My sense of this, though, is that this sort of thing ultimately distracts from unrestrained enjoyment of the experience through the senses of the right brain. Such overtly complex and complicated presentation can become a subject of conversation and, through that, ignite the left brain to further analyze the "how are they doing that?" rather than simply remaining immersed in the experience.

Once awakened, 'tis difficult to put that rascally left brain back to sleep.

Keep presentation simple. Save the complexity for the timing, for reveals, for a moment of exhilaration, for a finale or shock or surprise. But keep the experience simple to appreciate and enjoy.

Experiential
Messaging

I t was July 2012, and I was immersed in the redesign of
an annual "destination" event for an iconic California
institution of national legacy and global presence.
This was an opportunity to acutely focus my methodologies on refreshing a powerful brand of legacy while
articulating the evolutionary metamorphoses under
which this institution was going, in leadership, mission,
form, and function. A transformation was being completed, resulting in a more powerful, more effective, and
relevant organization, poised and prepared to make a
sweeping expansion and intensification in the level of
engagement with their surrounding communities.

I live for this stuff.

Experiential messaging

Connecting message at profound, emotional levels
through experience.

I talk about this, I teach workshops on this, I thrive on
this. Finding the pathway, the words, format, rhythm,
the way past preconception through the daily deluge of
data descending on all of us and our audiences day by
day, and connecting.

Connecting.

Imagine an experience that honors leadership, articulates vision, engages emotionally and viscerally, incites
passion and connects with an audience...all without
speeches. None were used at that event in 2012.
Everything was communicated through art in its many
forms: theatre, music, movement, imagery...

On that night we had an audience that mostly consisted of people involved in the work of the institution for years, even decades. There was nothing new to say to them; they entered the space almost out of obligation, not expecting anything they had not previously experienced. Those preconceptions had to be liberated and the individual impassioned anew.

Another part of the audience was fresh on the scene, not consciously connected to the legacy, though compassionate and committed to making a difference in the world being inherited. These men and women exited the experience at the end of the evening fired up; personally embracing the shared mission and seeking a place in it.

How did we do this?

We threw out all that had gone before, holding a virtual open audition for new and effective ways of delivering message and coming up with an immersive experience for a new age and attitude.

Back in the day, I began to refer to creation of an immersive experience to communicate message and connect audience to an institution "experiential messaging." I thought I'd invented that term; it's possible I heard it somewhere thirty years ago and adopted it. Either way, this term is bandied about these days by everyone from guerilla marketers passing out energy drink samples on the street, to those who actually do create fully immersive, messaging experiences.

What makes it experiential messaging?

The message is delivered *through* the experience rather than at it or in it.

Through the experience.

The integrity of this term is important to me, as I strongly believe in the power of shared personal experience. Power to motivate and inspire, power to challenge and engage, power to dissipate fatigue and familiarity and reawaken energy and vigor. Sure, being handed a box of mints on the street is an experience. It is not, however, immersive, nor is the messaging experiential.

To be effective, the crucial pieces are:

• Catching the audience off guard (liberating preconception).

• Surprising without shocking, taking them a tad off balance (comfortable disorientation).

Then, in the case of what we built for that night in San Francisco, creating the messaging experience such that it is artistic and stunning, clear and articulate, deeply emotionally connective...and brief.

Our audiences are such that, if they trust that a bit of program will be brief and compelling, they will stay, watch, listen, and hear. If we are trusted, when the lights dim the audience is inclined to give it a chance before reaching for their iPhone or running to the lounge.

You've got to catch 'em before they tweet. Then they gotta tweet, or check-in, or pin, or whatever the platform of the moment demands. Give them a reason to hang in; reward them with something to say or share.

- The messaging must be quick, focused, pithy, and relevant.
- And the food's gotta be great.
- And there must be plenty of time to socialize throughout the experience.
- And…the audience must know that the evening will end at a decent hour.

It will be over before the audience is ready for it to be over ("Always leave 'em wanting more"—P.T. Barnum), and it will be a complete, accessible, complex experience.

I shared the specifics and particulars of that 2012 production and narrative with one of my most respected clients, and he asked to join my production team for the night. That was a powerful compliment from a respected perfectionist, and I was thrilled to have him there.

Broadcasting live events

In the context of stadium or outdoor spectacles of most any sort, I believe the best seats are always in the house. I believe this is our responsibility to the audience. To my mind, the creation of live experience is, with integrity, focused on those physically present to absorb and appreciate—to experience—the full force of what is taking place on the stage, field, arena, or lagoon. The cameras are there to share what can be shared within the limits of their medium. They are there to archive, record, and communicate to the remote audience some sense of the high moments, the spectacle.

However, the inherent limitations of cameras, video, and film stand ineradicably in the way of actually communicating the experience. One simply cannot deliver the same, visceral rush to a remote audience that can be given to those present. Therefore, I believe that the audience for which perfection of pure experience can be given deserves to be given it.

This means, then, that the experience of the live audience is sacrosanct.

For the experiences I have produced with my creative teams, this has meant no cameras on the field, with no visible technology between the eyes of the audience and the action taking place before them. Nothing to activate the left brain, leaving the right to absorb experience without analysis. As camera and video technology has evolved, this has become far easier to accomplish with greater throws and the use of micro, suspended cameras that are virtually invisible.

I am distracted by close-ups of field performers. I don't need to see the individual smiling faces so much as to become connected and engaged by the choreographed movements on, across, and around the field. (Rock concerts are a different thing...we want to see faces and their fingers on the instruments.) Ergo, as I create live experience my focus is on the audience in the stadium (or wherever) along with the pure integrity of that experience. Then, once that is designed, I turn to the photographers and videographers to design pathways and angles that can best support them in their supplementary and archival mission.

Creative Catalyst

These spectacles are not designed for television!

Or so I've been known to posit.

As I will break down later in Chapter 16, Case Studies, the opening ceremonies for the London Olympics were specifically designed for broadcast; the audience in the stadium was clearly secondary. If those individuals did not pay attention to what was displayed on the screens, much of what was taking place in the stadium (or any of the multiple remote locations outside) would simply be lost. They would be unable to follow the (albeit loose) unfolding narrative.

So what is the reality here? What is acceptable? Can we augment without distracting? How much distraction is acceptable? More importantly, how much distraction is inevitable, and what is the tradeoff? What is being lost, and is it a bad thing? Even if it is a bad thing, is it going to be lost anyway?

I have the sense I may not be completely happy with the answer.

This was the subject of a conversation I had with one of my own mentors, Roberta Perry, an iconic maven of the themed entertainment industry. She was saying how much, despite her dedication to the integrity of the live experience, she enjoyed the broadcast of the London ceremonies quite largely due to their being designed and produced for television. Acknowledging that this is counter to her own philosophy, she said—enthusiastically—that she had had a great experience.

"I couldn't be there, so the broadcast was great for me…"

We both sort of lightheartedly grumbled about this. Still, its benefits must be acknowledged and faced. She raised the example of "back in the day," when people would attend baseball games with transistor radios at their ear throughout the play, giving them information they couldn't get from their seat.

Well, that was a long time ago, so this isn't a new thing, actually. Now, with smartphones people can get all sorts of stats, data, and visual information on their handheld screens. I believe this actually does enhance their enjoyment of the activity unfolding physically right before them.

I don't know that I like where this is going...

A sporting event, though, is not a storytelling spectacle; there is no narrative. And while games can be viscerally experienced during the high points, the digital data augmentation doesn't distract from anything as there is nothing to distract from.

We laughed (a little bitterly) at the fact that, "Well, there's purity and integrity of the experience...and then there's business." When push comes to shove, the producers and those looking to profit from the show or spectacle are going to want the greatest return on the investment.

Uh-oh. Show / Business.

So, what's the challenge here?

To create experience so intense and compelling that the technology in one's hand is forgotten? Even for a moment? I mean, we aren't going to keep screens of any size out of the room, so as crafters of live experience how do we address this?

I developed an experience for a major milestone in the history of an iconic institution in San Francisco (*see Chapter 17: The Call*). It took place indoors with an attendance around 500, and I doubt a single person in attendance was without a smartphone. I had a lot to communicate in the messaging of this experience, and we created a program with no speeches. It was all done theatrically.

In the attempt to address techno-addiction, we created four very short vignettes that were powerful and evocative, packed with intense visual and aural cues that delivered profound messages via oblique pathways. My goal was to help the audience forget the technology in the hand or pocket for those few moments and immerse them in experience. There was plenty of time between the theatrical segments for the talking, networking, eating, drinking...and, now, texting, tweeting, and Facebook-ing.

So what does this mean for what I define as the integrity of the live experience? What will we lose, and is there a way around it? How will we evolve our craft and ensure that being physically present in the audience is the prime spot for an experience, rather than being technologically, remotely connected to it?

What keeps tugging at the back of my mind is the Opening Ceremonies for the 1992 Barcelona Olympics. That archer. Jaw-dropping athleticism and art, all at once.

I saw it on television.

The
Creative Process

W hat is the nature of creativity? Where do great ideas come from? I didn't even attempt to analyze my own creative process for some time. That is probably largely due to the fact that I didn't even realize I had one. Nor did I work in an environment that embraced creativity. I was in politics and corporate communications for many years until I was advised and encouraged by an insightful VP and mentor to "stay with me as long as you like, but I think you should go out and do this thing you are so good at doing!"

In San Francisco, I had been loaned by the phone company to City Hall for a succession of big cere-monial productions at the behest of the late Steve Silver (creator of *Beach Blanket Babylon*—one of the longest-running theatrical productions in the world at the time). I served as his assistant producer on these spectacles. Steve had discerned something in me that I'd never really thought about—a complexity of thought, a geometric sense of time and space, and the crucial absence of the "limitation of possibility" gene.

After several successive periods of me being away from the office to work with Steve on a Fleet Week, a royal visit, or the Super Bowl Ceremony, my mentor took me to lunch and gifted me with the freedom to remain there as long as I wanted, but with the encouragement to follow my own path. "Success isn't always found in the board-room…" was a truth to which I'd never been enlightened.

Finding my own way

Previously, when my own inspiration blindsided me with an idea, I would embrace and augment it. I would take it as far as I could, just to see what it might become. I'd never actually paid attention to when nor how the seeds of that inspiration may have been planted, how research and study was surreptitiously done by my subconscious, and how my brain worked to massage an idea before revealing it to my frontal lobes.

As this new career grew, my opportunity was helping others find and define their vision. I used my own creativity as a tool to make it come to pass, keeping it aligned with a mission or goal while taking the germ of a vision to a place even the client may not have foreseen.

A fine line to walk, assessing how much of oneself to infuse or offer in creating experience. Ultimately, my enthusiasm and passion usually led me to offer it all, tempering as I go, reining in the ideas that were just too big or too out-there rather than restraining myself from the outset, offering simply what was expected. There are plenty of creators, though, who make fantastic livings by delivering what's expected.

I was fortunate to come up against a catalyzing experience—an epiphany of sorts—back in the '90s that gave me the opportunity to truly appreciate and realize how my own creativity worked. I had been brought on as creative director for a landmark national industrial theatre production company based in NYC. Their pitch to me was that they'd experienced my work, seen what I could create, and wanted that as part of their arsenal.

There was one problem: the only people who were allowed client contact at the beginning of a project were the sales people.

So, the account representatives would go out on a call, meet the client, get their experience of the client's vision, and come back to the office. I would gather with them around the table in the conference room while they told me what (they thought) the client wanted. Then they'd sit back and wait for my wonderful, creative ideas on how to execute, as though creative concepts were akin to toothpaste one might simply squeeze out of a tube.

I lasted a month.

Lovely people, but that's not how I work.

Since then, I have meticulously examined my process and learned to protect and nurture that process in order to deliver experience well beyond expectation. There are lots of ways of going about this, but here are some ideas that work for me.

What are the outcomes?

My own first step is in the exploration of what is wanted, to be communicated, to be seen, heard, and experienced. What is the message or call to action, the fable, parable, or simple lesson to be articulated and communicated? What result do we seek?

Interview the client one-on-one

For me, there is nothing of greater value than the subtextual information that can be gleaned in the first meeting with a client. It is during that first encounter, when the right questions are asked, that the nuance is most clear and the personal motivations and inspirations behind the official talk can come to light. This is where creative empathy and compassion become the rod and staff of the creative; this is where subtext and inadvertent communication can be perceived by the sensitive creative and woven into the process.

Don't get ahead of yourself

Meet before musing. Meet the client before brainstorming with collaborators or partners. Enter that first meeting cold, sans preconception, with no virtual "box" or budget in mind and learn. Listen.

Take what was learned in that first meeting and go experience the world with that filter. For one day or ten, see things through this new, borrowed lens. Take things in, notice things differently. Just as the guy who's recently bought a new car suddenly notices the same model everywhere, the sensitive creative will receive impressions and data, visuals and experience in a slightly new and pivotally relevant way.

Don't try to offer ready-made solutions. My practice is to never present concepts for sale. (There are rare exceptions…money does talk, after all!) Rather, I present and offer myself and my body of work as my recommendation and market the opportunity to collaborate and create something compelling, resonant, and of the client. I do not sell concepts created in a vacuum of what might work. Rather, I guarantee that, working with me in partnership, the result will be something powerful and borne of the interaction, not something taken off a shelf, dusted off, and sold.

Perceive the space

Know the venue, theatre, or arena. There have been some spectacles I've created that were initially inspired by the place itself in which they were produced.

I once had the experience of conducting a live interview before an audience with Yves Pepin, the world-class creator of spectacle, founder of ECA2 in Paris and who, among a host of other once-in-a-lifetime spectacles, created the Eiffel Tower Millennium show. At one point I asked him where he found his inspiration. In his eloquent, French-accented English, he explained he would go and sit in the space until the space spoke to him. Whether that was an existing stadium or venue, or an empty desert where the facility was yet unbuilt, he would listen to the land or the architecture and await inspiration.

To that, if the planned experience is to be site-specific, it's important to go see and experience a given space before writing for it. For me, the enhancement to my creative process cannot be over-valued.

Anything goes...at first

I prefer to ignore budget during the first pass at concept development, to let ideas flow freely, in my own mind or in creative conversation, unhindered by any reality. When working with a team of professional craftspeople—technicians, artists, talent, musicians, designers—I begin with an unlimited "blue sky" approach.

Were budget not an issue and we could do anything, what would we do...how best might we tell this story?

Through my own experience, I believe that a far better idea can come from an unrestrained process than might be realized by attempting to develop a concept and physically articulate narrative within a pre-defined "budget box." Taking a magnificent, insightful storytelling concept and, through the alchemy of collaborative chiseling and massage, bringing it into alignment with financial constraints can greatly heighten the quality and innovation that comes into play. We can realize unleashed—though workable—creativity while protecting the integrity of the concept.

I find there's a lot more love and engagement on the part of the entire team and process when everything's been expressed and explored and the Big Idea has been embraced. The risk of savage dogfights over resources is largely alleviated when the entire team is working to protect this big idea to which each has already contributed and is invested. The net result is a more cohesive team and a powerful, compelling experience.

Be prepared for some surprises, though. Even better, prepare your executives and clients for this process before you begin sharing the step-by-step process of evaluating concepts coming out of that process. I once neglected to fully prepare my client team for the possibility of ridiculously high numbers attached to concepts as the bid proposals arrived for a project budgeted at $7—12 million. When a bid concept priced at $37 million hit the table, I thought we were about to lose one of the more fragile members in paroxysms of apoplexy!

Oops. Clue 'em in. Early.

For some, this may seem a waste of time. I think different.

Trust yourself

Know that the answers, the concepts, and the ideas will come. And relax. Keep your eye on the goal, the experience wanted, and the response envisioned; that is the most effective, reliable way to ensure success. Not blindly, mind you. Listening remains a key component of creativity and creative collaboration.

Team creativity

In my experience, one of the best ways to get the best work out of the best people is to engage early. A journey of a thousand ideas begins with a single conversation. The time to begin to involve one's team—even one's prospective team—is at the very beginning.

I know that my own muse lives deep within me and works in mysterious ways, sharing inspiration and ideas on her schedule and with her unique styles. (Mine is definitely a she. I don't know how I know, I just know.) With that, when I have the first meeting with a prospective client or on a possible project, I listen with focus as the vision is expressed.

The idea machine kicks right into gear.

I take that knowledge and hand it off to her. Sometimes she comes right back, even during that meeting, with concept possibilities; sometimes it takes a few days or even weeks...which can be indulged, given enough time before deadline. Ideas start dropping into my creative inbox; I examine and explore them, and a concept begins to come together for me.

Most often, as I'm "looking the other way" and working on something else, the other thing percolates. Simmering, it becomes a repository of possibility, a subtle filter through which I see and experience day-to-day without the pressure to apply or do anything with the oblique input.

Then, one day—Boom! There it is!

At the same time my thoughts begin converging on how to create the experience, I often recognize just whom among the vast constellation of creative and technical professionals I've come to know are likely to be most well-suited or of greatest potential for contributing and collaborating on this particular project. I call them and share where I am—long before I may need answers and ideas from them.

Long before the time comes when we'll be needing to gather and work, I find that planting concept seeds early offers that same subliminal dynamic for the other professional craft and tech people who will be joining me to make this happen. A brief conversation at this very early outset of a project or show, simply planting seeds of ideas, offers a subtle and profound power to the interim time before the work actually starts.

The seeds grow in different ways, nurtured and affected by the mind in which they've been planted. I suppose it's similar to planting flowers in a row. Each bloom is just that much different having had a little different light, a little different water, been pollinated differently, or having had a chrysalis attached at some point. It's not until all the blooms have been gathered that the facets and textures of the bouquet are able to be grasped and appreciated as more than the sum total of the parts.

Just as these concepts develop differently within the composer, the set and lighting designers, the costumer, the choreographer, and so on, sometimes the concept itself evolves through outside influence—be it calendar, budget, client relationships, whatever.

The point is that when we gather to flesh out the actual experience, everyone at the table has differently-generated ideas to share, ideas about which each are excited. These ideas grew peacefully and under far less pressure than might otherwise exist were I to have waited until it was time to start briefing and begin. Knowing where an idea began and seeing where it may have arrived by the time we meet offers numerous new possibilities for where it can be taken. I believe the projects and shows I've managed in this way have reflected the work of the muses in unforeseeable ways.

Early conversations with each of your prospective principal team members pays off handsomely at showtime. While I am familiar with many a producer who resists taking such time at the outset, in my own experience it involves less time overall and can yield far more interesting and compelling results when the muse is treated with due respect.

Creative Catalyst

Taking the time up front to share my own ideas of where a vision can be taken has, in my experience, come back to me and to the project tenfold. Don't wait until the answers and solutions are defined and needed; spread the inspiration wide and have so much more to work with when it comes back.

The net result of this process is that, at the other end, one has the best sense of the principles, ethos, creativity, and perspective of the contributing contractors, vendors, or teammates from and through the genesis. We end up with a better concept to whittle, knowing a lot more about the potential members of the production team.

Eschew shyness and caution. This is an exhilarating tightrope; imagination your net. There is no falling.

We create better experience from the limb than on the ground, without risk.

Blue sky ideation: charrettes

The pheromonal element to collaboration

Project: New feature for an established theme park.

Setting: Large square table in a big conference room. Nine brilliant people (plus me)—few of whom had met before—and all of whom were gathered to come up with a Brand New Concept.

Process: Charrette.

Format: Two full days of intensive ideation, followed by two weeks of fleshing out the concept, drawing and specifying, at the end of which we were to make our pitch to the client.

Each individual on our team of ten had been hand-picked. The mission was a massive, super secret creative project for a certain large entertainment company. Very few of us had met one another until immediately prior to the launch of the process. Yet from our fortnight of collaboration came some of the most powerfully compelling, realistic, and feasible original creative concepts any of us have had the privileged experience of being a part for quite some time. The atmosphere throughout the entire arc was high-energy, full of engagement, respect, acknowledgment, and enthusiasm as ideas were born, shared, augmented, and articulated.

Approaching showtime, as passionate as each of us were for this entire far-greater-than-the-sum-of-its-parts experience, we were apprehensive as to how this would all be received by The Client. That particular client was as discerning and rare to impress as they come, setting standards across the industries in which we work. The overriding goal when presenting was to at least meet expectation, with perhaps an elusive dream of surpassing them...though with no delusions.

As we worked, as our project took magnificent shape, we began to fully appreciate what we had and became proud and excited by our own work. "What if...this really blows away the client?"

Well. We did. Met and exceeded...

How did this happen? In a word: *charrette*.

What the heck is a charrette?

Born of the architectural communities in 19th century France, a *charrette* was the physical cart in which the work of architectural students was collected on the day of an exhibition. During the mid-1900s the word came to mean an extended working meeting in which all stakeholders gather to resolve conflicts and map solutions.

In the theme park industry, and in its most pure form, the charrette has become a multi-day meeting (generally two days, though sometimes more) of a disparately backgrounded, differently experienced, and differently focused group of professionals, artists, producers, and stakeholders. Sometimes it's augmented with peripheral professions or members representing audience demographics. They gather to envision possibility without boundaries for a park, land, experience, resort, destination, or experience phenomenon of any type.

Done before the application of budget and time to a given project, this "blue sky" session can uncover vast possibilities previously unimagined as differing points of view, likes and dislikes, personal histories, and visions are gathered and mixed in this "pheromonal crucible" of minds and imaginations.

(Pheromonal? What's that even mean?)

We'll get to that.

The first charrette of my career in these industries was run by Phil Hettema of The Hettema Group. Through that intense and fruitful experience the high standard was set for me. That was twenty years ago at the beginning of a project, now fully realized, that is now ranked as one of the best theme parks in the world. So, that's my model of how this might best be done.

It can be an expensive process, though, involving fees, travel, meals, and lodging (generally at an "off-site" location in order to prevent or at least minimize distraction and keep focus on the project). All in the name of thoroughness and vast freedom of imaginations, sure, but also serving to deliver the best return on investment.

Charrette vs brainstorm

The phenomenon of the charrette is something that rarely happens in an agency. Time and money usually stand in the way. In agencies and corporations, this process has effectively been pared down and optimistically labeled a brainstorm—maybe a couple of hours to a day in a conference room, banging out ideas under the pressure of an immediate deadline. Not ineffective, certainly, and definitely far better than not doing something at all. This creative forum differs from the charrette in that:

- It is far shorter.

- There is no "downtime" or space for meditation and cogitation for ideas to simmer and for the subconscious muse to do her work.

- People tend to enter and leave based on needs of projects and/or callings that are "just down the hall..."

- It is not unheard of for participants to call-in or attend for only what they consider a "relevant section" of the conversation.

- Often the entire process is conducted online:

one or two hours of collaborative dodgeball,
with ideas coming out of brilliant minds as
though from a circle of batting cages.

While many great things do come out of brainstorming—and this is not to disparage a very necessary and
proven productive process, the results of which make
thousands of clients a year very happy—there is no
substitute for the charrette.

And that is why the secret project charrette I described
was so phenomenal...so pheromonally phenomenal. The
fact that the agency involved in our project took a look
at the stakes and decided to invest in this process was
eminently forward-thinking and delivered a result that
had the client in candidly-expressed awe.

We flew them in from NYC, Chicago, Orlando, Los
Angeles, and St. Paul to meet in San Francisco at a relatively pastoral non-office facility, surrounded by trees
and ocean. Our first experience was one of discovery
and inspiration as we took the group to an immersive
spot to which none had ever been. Thus was provided a
shared experience of unique discovery, as each individual connected with something different and came
away excited and revitalized by that discovery.

The afternoon involved an intense download of all the
background information—the research, the mission and
vision of the client, all the data, the work that had been
done to date, the mandate, and our scope. Then we
were assigned homework for individual contemplation
to be shared on Day Two. We had time in the evening to
spend alone, to ruminate on what we'd seen and heard
on that first day and let silence do its work.

The second day was an intense and organized, wonderfully productive flurry of ideas and artwork. At the end of the day the walls and table were covered with concept art, features, and components of a vast and disparate family of concepts which, woven together, might truly manifest something never before seen—a destination that reflected and drew an evolving world and a participatory tapestry of human cultural existence.

And yet, the true value of the two days was realized in the days that followed.

Having met and come to know one another at some level, having worked and collaborated in person with one another, the opportunity in what I call "pheromonal collaboration" was fully realized.

Having everyone in the same place at the same time, hearing and responding to the same things—each from their own experience and POV—having each person able to experience the reactions and points of view of the others while observing various responses to the same input, ensured a strong sense of team and awareness of the issues.

With no in-and-out, no one jumping in to participate only in a given area of expertise, we were able to tap into the experience of each individual beyond their core capabilities or talents. Some of our most thoughtful, compelling, and exciting ideas for technical components, for instance, did not come from our digital and technology experts. Some of our most accessible experiences for children came from the mind of a person who happens to not have any. And so forth...

Creative Catalyst

The whole person—the entire team together—at the table at the same time for everything made our subsequent collaboration in bringing these ideas to articulation and definition fantastically smooth. Not that it was all easy, mind you. There was sweat and pressure aplenty. But the massive amount that was accomplished in a short period of time between ideation and concept presentation—the depth and breadth of concepts realized and expressed—was breathtaking, for us and for the client.

It was productive and exhilarating; we all were and still are appreciative of the foresight and investment outside the paradigm this company chose to make. This is not something that happens every day or could be possible with every project.

It's about the audience, after all

Audience expectation is defined by, and thus limited to, what audience members believe is possible. As creators of experience the responsibility is ours to exceed such expectation and take our audience to unanticipated places, to offer unforeseen experiences.

This does not necessarily mean an increase in magnitude, however. Indeed, it can often mean the opposite. Sometimes, taking a quieter road, one of less "production" (but with high standards) and stronger substance, can result in a far more powerful experience.

Never, though, am I happy with simply meeting audience expectation. In many instances and contexts, in fact, audiences subconsciously accept and "expect" to make excuses for substandard work...

- Well, they're on a small budget...
- Well, the weather...
- Well, it's their first time trying that...
- Well, it's hard to deliver to an audience in a stadium/park/rooftop...
- And the worst: Well, it's for charity.

Anathema.

None of these are acceptable. This is what creativity and commitment is all about. Respect your audience and never give them a reason to excuse what you create, be it a one-off, a theatrical run, or a permanently-installed attraction. Audience first.

Tools are for storytelling

We need to be current on the most recently-developed or under-development techniques for projection, movement, sound, and staging. We are dealing with new generations of audiences who are far more sophisticated in terms of "show" than in the past. Between Google, all the entertainment channels, websites, platforms, and feeds, as well as the many other ways in which people absorb information, the understanding, appreciation, and expectation of show and show effects has been raised simply in the course of daily life.

This is good; this pushes us to extend our own reach. What it also does is place the challenge of surpassing expectation back onto the storytelling...where it should be. In many cases our audience will be just as savvy as to what is technologically possible as are we. No problem. we are storytellers, creators of compelling experience.

In immersive storytelling—experiential messaging—the key to compelling isn't the inclusion of technology and effects. Rather, it is the nimble and creative use of such things to the point that they become invisible, and it is their contribution to the narrative that brings the gasp to the lips and the heart to the throat.

So...create, already!

Rediscovery

What I like most about what I do is finding ways to captivate an audience with a story they believe they already know...to engage them in rediscovery.

Rediscovery, as I define and strive to create it, is an experience more subtly profound and nuanced, running deeper than recall or remembering. Most simply, rediscovery is created through sublime evocation while memory is stirred by articulate reminder—two very different things.

This is why I so eagerly embrace opportunities that come my way for writing, staging, and telling of oft-told stories—taking cultural legends, myths, and traditional folk tales that are multiple generations old and weaving them into ceremonies, theatrical shows, or presentations for multigenerational audiences. Finding ways to give an old story new resonance with today's aspirational, global citizens while maintaining the integrity sought by the elder segment of a given audience is the welcome creative challenge for the entire team.

Burnishing the patina of an old story and helping it evolve to emerge in unexpected ways, taking a more circuitous path toward denouement such that the reward of recognition takes on greater, more expansive power and release, are the challenges that—as they become realized—excite and empower the creative teams long before audiences get to experience them.

That is the process that compels and fulfills me.

Gathering a creative production team of artists, designers, technicians, engineers, composers, choreographers, logisticians, cultural experts, and anthropologists—even the occasional dramaturg—and studying the kernel of the story is where this energy begins for me.

Exploring together the possibilities of a story, creating a backstory or peripheral bit that can be obliquely expressed, deepening the connection by subtly opening an emotional door in the heart of each audience member...these are the little mysteries that, as solved, become the compelling beats of a well-told story.

This is how I've come to create terms such as successive revelation, subliminal engagement, comfortable disorientation. Give the story to the audience in such a way that it becomes personal to each individual. Evoke imagery and motivation, hint at possibility, craft the unfolding of the story in such a way that each person is psychically seeking, virtually leaning forward and reaching out for the next revelation, the next step, with breathless, sotto voce gasps of recognition as conclusion nears.

This must be built with a team that is willing to go there with me—willing to not know how we're going to tell this

The Creative Process

83

story when we first gather. As I share for the first time the vision I have for a given show, spectacle, or experience, what gives me the most pleasure is to see professional eyes around the table light up with inspiration as the initial concept is shared. Seeds of ideas are planted in those who will ultimately create dimension and bring the story to life. Personal investment is made on the part of each player, and the dynamic that begins up front will yield idea after passionately collaborative idea as the process unfolds.

Essentially, every story I tell has to become personal to me, or I cannot make it personal to the audience. So, yes, sometimes there may be a bit of weeping. This is me, after all. People who know me well know that I am wired to feel and to offer others those feelings.

After all these years at the fair, I'm glad to know that I have not (yet?) become jaded. I consider myself lucky to have this healthy, compassionate inner child, to carry within me this unfiltered heart...as it is this heart through which I find each discrete pathway to story.

Simply put: When I can move myself, I can move you. That is my method. For this wet-eyed trait I do take no small ration of good-natured ribbing from colleagues and crew who work often with me. Though when the voice shakes a bit in the telling of the tale and tears hint at appearance, we know we're on track.

It's a dependable barometer.

We can show people images of something happy and make them smile or even cheer at the recognized, remembered event or moment. We can show people pictures of very sad things and give them a sense of sadness. We can show them images of places they've been, things they've done, people they've known and elicit fond, happy, or wistful memories...creating an excellent and memorable show experience.

Yet we can ease all the way into their heads, plumb the protected or even forgotten depths such that they are no longer seeing through their eyes, but are rediscovering something precious and wonderful within themselves. We can take them to another plane of experience...and when that is accomplished, as this shared experience becomes uniquely personal, the house, arena, or stadium becomes filled with a different sort of silence. Palpable silence, almost velvet-like, as each person in the audience privately experiences this thing that belongs only to themselves.

Just for a moment. A shared, intimate moment all the more powerful in that throughout the space each are having their own unique experience, en masse. Taking an audience to that place keeps my own heart alive, my muse nimble, myself fulfilled. It is the pursuit and sharing of that moment that keeps me inspired...and keeps me working!

Some years ago we created a thirteen-city tour of a full theatrical production for a well-known university development campaign. Believe me, this alumni body knows everything about their school and could call it up and quote it at will. Crafting an experience that took these men and women all the way back to discovery was the daunting and appealing challenge embraced.

The challenge was met, and with emotional connection exceeded. We raised over $1 billion and, as I characterize it, "...left rooms full of weeping millionaires in our

Creative Catalyst

wake." An apt enough description (though they weren't actually all millionaires).

For our closing celebration, before the team disbanded and went on to other projects, I wrote an epic poem of commemoration, the final stanza of which strives to articulate that moment when we truly have a trusting audience in our intimate grasp. I think it may apply to any and all of us who do what we do:

> But there was a moment, in every city
> When what we did went to profound from pretty.
> When guests became silent, when hearts skipped a beat,
> When each person settled more into the seat.
> The air in the room became quieter, still,
> And breath was abated as hearts took the thrill.
> That's when we touched them, that's when we knew
> We'd delivered completely on our mission, true.
> No one will ever accomplish again
> What we have given to those where we've been...

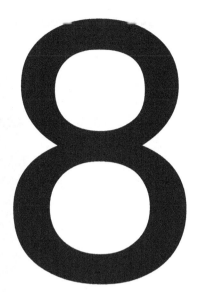

Leadership

Creatives can be led. Creatives can be managed. Creatives cannot be controlled.

That being said, the opposite of "control" is not necessarily "out of control." Creative leadership, and the leadership of creatives, is dependent on these critical qualities:

1. Authentic respect
2. Ongoing & focused listening
3. Passion for the work
4. Humility
5. Exhibited trust
6. Willingness to teach and to learn

Gone are the days of old-fashioned, last-century, top-down management styles, to the confused frustration of many a managing director, creative director, general manager, project manager, chairman, or CEO. No longer can one direct or lead from a position of power, for that "power" is now largely irrelevant. Expecting to be followed, heard, or even respected by the creative team because of one's title and body of work simply won't cut it with today's evolved creatives.

Leadership has evolved; managing creativity is, most effectively and productively, inherently and fundamentally collaborative.

Before going into specifics of each leadership quality, let's take a look at one of the most effective models of such collaborative team-building, inspiration, and work: the theatre.

In theatre, everyone on the team has an opinion and tends to share it. All members of the team share a passion for what they do and for connecting the story with the audience. The most successful directors listen to—and hear—everyone, then make a decision. Once the director's decision is made, the team then aligns and supports the director in the vision, the course, the production. Each has been heard, the decision has been made—onward to storytelling victory!

Having been heard, each individual now has a sense of being appreciated and respected, gaining investment in the final product. This is collaboration at its most basic and simplest...and a resonant model.

Today, a creative leader, or one who leads creatives, must be a part of the team. The clearest analogy is to "sit on the same side of the table" as the rest of the team.

So, the six principles:

1.Authentic respect

A leader must truly respect the team.

This means knowing who each individual is: names, origins, backgrounds, strengths, weaknesses, and passions. When launching a project with a new team, a powerful first step is to informally "interview" each member, asking open questions and hearing the answers...answers that often reveal more about the individual than may lie on the surface.

Avoid being "all business," as people respond better and are far more creative once there is some level of connection between everybody. Creatives today (all people, actually) respond more fully and engage more completely when they sense a connection...and this cannot be faked.

To respect someone you work with, you must know that person. Such respect for the team engenders reciprocal respect for the leader. Team members feel seen and heard, thus respected. Thus willing to jump in and contribute without hesitation. Thus giving the process the benefit of the full wealth of talent and creativity.

2. Ongoing & focused listening

There is no rush.

Creativity takes the time it takes. Communication takes the time it takes. So listen. Fully. Be focused on what is being said and save the evaluation of what you're hearing and the formulation of your response until the entire idea or concept being shared is articulated and on the table.

You know what we're saying. It takes discipline to shut down the voice in your head, the voice that's already evaluating and preparing a response, and simply hear everything being said. Countless are the times that the most salient of points is made at the end of an idea, share, or rant.

Let 'em talk. Hear all of what is being said before you say anything.

Listen. Think. Speak.

Then...

Give. Them. Time.

There is a method, a great rule of thumb, taken from documentary filmmaking. When interviewing a subject on camera, a question is asked, then answered. It's a natural instinct, when the interviewee has finished responding, to immediately jump in with another question, to fill the silence with something. However, if the interviewer exercises the discipline to remain silent, to consider what has just been shared, more often than not it is the interviewee who steps back in with more... and this "more" is usually the quote or the moment for which the segment is remembered. Sometimes such discipline can completely change the tone and tenor of an interview.

Try this in creative or management meetings. When someone makes a statement, responds to a question, or otherwise shares or contributes, take a breath before responding. Use that breath to consider what was just said in its entirety and in the context of the conversation. Look around the room and see who's bursting to contribute. If nothing else, it can make you look smarter!

And, amazingly, these brief pauses to think and consider can actually shorten the time needed to create or develop the perfect concept, as everyone at the table is spending more time thinking while they watch you!

Give it a go.

3. Passion for the work

A leader leads with passion.

This also cannot be faked. One who is not passionate about creating experience cannot inspire passion in others. Above all, it is the passion of the leader that fuels everything else in the process. It is one's passion that most effectively inspires others to invest fully, to participate unhesitatingly, to do their best work in support of the vision.

Articulating your passion, sharing and showing your enthusiasm, commitment, and personal fulfillment derived from the work is, if not the only way, by far the most effective way of gaining the respect and investment of the team.

If you're doing it for the money, go do something else. While it is possible to recruit creatives to the team with money, that's not what will engage them. It is the identification of a passionate person of like-mind that will engage and result in the best work. People may take a job for the money. But they will be of far more value when their passion for the work, the craft, the project, and for connecting with the audience is met and matched by the leader. They'll fight to return and work again with that leader.

Passion. Share it.

4. Humility

The leader need not know everything.

The leader must know how to learn, get, or find everything. Leadership is not about telling others what to do; it is about inspiring others to do their best work, even inspiring them to discover new levels of creative insight within themselves.

Letting go any preconceptions about being the leader and embracing the fact that one does not know everything gives the rest of the team the opportunity to contribute appreciable value. Most people enjoy being able to enlighten or expand the knowledge of the leader through the creative process.

Humility in leadership inspires increased self-worth on the part of the team members.

5. Trust, exhibited

Trust your people to do their jobs.

Be clear about what is wanted and needed, the parameters and responsibilities. Be sure that the scope and deadlines are understood and agreed. Then, get out of the way and allow the person to work in the manner in which they do their best work, personally responsible for the result.

When building a team and launching a project, my approach is to:

- Lay out the job responsibilities and be sure they are understood.

- If appropriate, share the process or method by which I would accomplish the job, leaving plenty of room for the person accepting the responsibilities to use any process they feel is most appropriate. It might be a combination of mine and theirs, or just theirs.

- All I ask is that, if and when it becomes apparent that a deadline may not be met or a result not achieved, the individual come to me with the problem so we can solve it.

- And, in seeking the solution, I usually ask the person what they see as the best option.

- Then I can say, "Why not go ahead and do that, then?"

Permission and trust. Can't beat 'em.

6. Willingness to teach and to learn

With this idea of trust in mind, a confident leader must be willing to share the how and why of their own methodologies and practices while keeping the door wide open to learn from those they are teaching or leading.

Learning to question without challenging keeps information and insight flowing in both directions. The simple fact that someone else has a way of doing things different than the way you might have gone about it does not mean the other way is wrong or worse (or better). It's just different.

Creative Catalyst

Be willing to evolve one's own methodologies, to embrace the new without needing to jettison the tried and true. Continuous and ongoing refreshing of one's perspective will keep a long-serving leader fresh, relevant, sought after, and respected.

Remember: Creatives are managed through passion, not by directive.

Shoulder to shoulder

Becoming and being a leader does not require one to know everything. The best, most effective leaders are those who recognize their own limitations, know who can get things done, motivate others to do their best work, and acknowledge those who deliver.

A leader must know what they want to accomplish— what they want their audience to feel, what effect they want to have on the audience. Then to gather those artists into a group that can gel as a team and create the thing...allowing that thing to organically reveal the path toward the vision.

The best course is to be open to what the process may reveal itself to be. Rather than sticking to a system or process that has worked before, perhaps reference past experience as a model or guideline while remaining prepared, nimble, and ready to adjust as the skills of the team come to light or the unique particulars of a given project manifest themselves.

While the official leader is responsible for delivering the result, product, or production, leadership can be found throughout any good team. Wielding one's leadership capabilities is about inspiring the best of people no matter where they fall within the hierarchy. One can lead from within a team or lead upwards from below. One can lead from another team. Leadership is not just a "boss" thing. In fact, a team in which every member has some of the qualities of leadership is probably a great team.

A team of leaders is a team of professionals who reach out to one another when they can be of help to each other. The spectrum of "Need some help with that?" to "Hey, can I run something past you?" is a continuum of learning and bonding situations, all of which will show up in the final product again and again.

A true leader sees no shame in not knowing how to do something. When presented with a task or situation that you're unsure of, call in the reinforcements! The sooner the leader throws open the door with "Who knows how to do…" the earlier potential resolutions to a given situation or problem are addressed and likely solved. Keeping information to yourself, "holding the cards close to your chest," undermines the strength and potential effectiveness of a team. Trust your team: share information.

I come to the table with my own systems and procedures, honed and evolved over the succession of projects delivered with these tools. Each time, though, I look at how others on my team might approach a given task or set of responsibilities to see if there might be something in their method that would enhance the effectiveness of how I am working. Not always, but every so often I see something in someone else's work tools that I can weave into my own. I then share this new idea with that individual.

Naturally, there are times I've tried something that looked good but turned out to be not as effective as a system I've already honed. No harm, no foul, but if you don't keep an eye out for new ideas the unique will ever be out of reach.

Gather your trusted team and dissect the problem, ask for suggestions from the perspectives of the individual team members, then take responsibility for the resulting course of action by making the decision. Leadership requires taking responsibility, showing respect and appreciation for the knowledge and skills of others while listening and making appropriate decisions. Hearing an idea from a team member and responding with "Okay, let's give that a shot..." could be followed up by vesting that individual with responsibility for applying the approach. "Adriana, why don't you oversee that, then? Keep me posted on how it's going." This is an opportunity to imbue strong trust between you and the team.

Of course there will be times when the proposed solution doesn't work out. Don't point fingers. Instead, respond along the lines of "Well, we learned that didn't work! Let's tackle it another way..." Keep Adriana on the project and partner with her to shepherd the problem all the way to resolution and completion. Give her the credit as it materializes.

Another opportunity for the leader to strengthen one's relationship with the team is to approach people for assistance in situations that may not be under their purview, but fall within their skill sets. Often people involved in production specialize at things they do in everyday life simply because they love doing them. If you've taken the time to know your people, you're more likely to know about these additional abilities.

Don't fake it

Production is no place for posers. Be open, share the problem, and the solution will become apparent. Share approbation and credit and your leadership will grow... and you'll experience a loyalty that cannot be bought. In doing this, you've shown the team that you trust them, will stand behind them, and are not one of those "producers" compelled to pose as though they know everything.

Who wants to know everything, anyway? There would be no surprises, no learning, and it is the daily and weekly learning that takes place on any project that keeps me interested and engaged. Embrace absence of knowledge as opportunity and possibility and empower your team with support for what they are becoming.

Collaboration at the Apple Store

During the financial crash of 2009, I was most fortunate to find myself immersed among a bunch of twenty-somethings at Apple SoHo. It was a golden time for that company and the perfect time for me. Where I first walked in to this sea of edgy youth thinking I'd never fit, I learned in short order that this was just the opportunity for me to completely recalibrate my own collaborative style—something of which I'd been proud and something I learned could be vastly revivified in that maelstrom of tech and humanity.

Creative Catalyst

No one knows everything on the floor at Apple, but together we knew it all. The context is one of ad hoc dynamic collaboration. Everyone is resource to each other, respect is paramount, and the fundamental skill—the basis of success in that place—is listening to one another, to the customer.

We each had our own ways of addressing a given problem; yet, with successive interactions each of our approaches evolved just a tad, time after time, as we collaborated with other specialists or Apple Geniuses on a given problem at hand.

We learned all the time, about the technology and about one another. The level of respect afforded every single team member was radically empowering; we each knew something the person next to us did not, and we each could learn something from that same person.

There was an inherent, healthy curiosity, an inquisitiveness among the team. "Who ARE you…?"

Make the workplace fun!

The morale of your team is your responsibility—100%.

Be it project or production team, theatrical company, business or corporation, morale amongst the troops directly affects everything you're trying to accomplish. This is the one place where trickle down is most acutely accurate—it all comes from the top.

We are making magic for our audiences, creating experiences that tell stories, engage, and compel. These experiences draw people in, open their hearts and imaginations, and take them to another place, another world, where physics are irrelevant and magic is possible—where imagination rules. (If this strikes you as crazy, then you are definitely in the wrong business.)

A workplace without levity and laughter will undermine the vision and diminish the effectiveness of your product or production—in both subtle and tangible ways. As leaders, it is our responsibility to see to it that everyone on our teams enjoys the work they are doing, that the late nights and weekends that inevitably become the rule rather than the exception are embraced out of enthusiasm, passion, and commitment, not through obligation or fear. We want positive and upbeat energy. We want proactive and productive action. We want an atmosphere of buoyant, confident exploration and innovative problem solving.

You want an amazing product? Nurture a strong sense of camaraderie and team. That must come from leadership. That is leadership.

It saddens me when I encounter a "creative" workplace that is quiet and somber, where people are afraid to venture their opinions for fear of reprisal or retribution, or are simply being ignored. I see this more often than I'd like, and I believe I can see the result in lackluster work from environments such as this.

Yes, this is a business. Show business. Note that the first word is "show"—it isn't "the business of show"— and show is the most important component. Show comes from passion, creativity, commitment, vision, and drive. The better our show, the better our business. The better our show, the more the marketing department has to sell, the better word of mouth, the more repeat business, the more kids will come away with eyes alight…and this latter is at the heart of what we are lucky enough to be doing for a living.

Do we not want our audiences to love it? Then, we'd better be loving the process by which we get there. Simply put, if laughter is not regularly heard in your workplace, something's wrong. If people walk around with brows knit and eyes downcast, you've got trouble.

How to address this? Simple.

Know and acknowledge your people. Let them know that you and they are on the same team, and that you are aware that the captain of the team does not score all the points. It is imperative that the leader know the members of the team as more than simply the offices they fill or titles each holds. These people come to the team for a reason, a personal reason, and it is the mandate of the leader to know from where the passion of each member arises. Passion for our work is vital.

A leader who does not know the names of every team member and what brings that person to the job is letting down all the stakeholders in a given project…and that includes the audience with which you are hoping to fill your seats and queues.

Know your people, your team. Know who they are, what inspires and impassions them. Meet their eyes as you pass in the hallway and never forsake the opportunity to simply say "hello." Creative and otherwise, human beings need to know they are seen and heard. If you want the best from your team, they must feel valued, acknowledged, and welcome to contribute, even outside an official realm of responsibility.

As leader, one must take most seriously the responsibility of seeing each person on your team and of being open and creating the opportunity to hear them. One never knows where the next good idea, the most creative solution, the best potential for growth and ROI will originate. Be sure to know everyone on your team. There is brilliance there that you very well may not yet know. Brilliance, value, and inspiration.

Nurture it.

That's our job. We are lucky to have it. Embrace the opportunity to be inspired by your teams as you seek to inspire them. 'Tis a rare and wonderful opportunity that will yield results in the hundredfold.

Transparency & inclusion

Western society and corporate culture continue to evolve into new methodological contexts. Raised expectations of transparency, participation, collaboration, and recognition of the inherent value of the individual are increasingly part and parcel of membership, stakeholder, or workforce in an association, organization, or business.

In my experience, the arrival of the millennium was a harbinger of a new, evolved way of thinking and communicating, born of a couple of generations of self-exploration and realization. From Timothy Leary to Arthur Janov, peyote and weed to LSD and ecstasy, Werner Erhard through Gordon Gekko to the new optimo-realists of Simon Sinek and Brené Brown, our culture has and continues to become more expectant of clarity and transparency.

Let's first address the term "millennial." Typically applied as a label for a specific age demographic, its usage has evolved. If anything, I see millennial as a point of view, a way of seeing things, a combination of aspiration, inquisitiveness, and a strong sense of one's value that pervades vast segments of society and culture. Not specific to any particular age or generation, this way of thinking is more broadly represented in exponentially greater segments of the professional workforce...who plan to continue working for some time to come.

Thus, it behooves those in leadership positions to embrace the evolution and factor consciousness of these perspectives into management and leadership techniques and styles that resonate and function effectively in the new world.

What does this mean? Listening.

In broad terms what this means is that the aged model of top-down leadership is dying on the vine of ineffectiveness. Executives and boards (especially of non-profits and increasingly so of corporations) can no longer expect membership, staff, or workforce to accept what was decreed in the privacy of the boardroom or back office.

People who have been immersed in transparency and open availability of information for the greater part of their lives are not willing to accept the traditional dictum and edict model anymore. Those affected by decisions expect to see the etymology behind these decisions and policies—to see, participate in, appreciate, and embrace the path by which they were reached. Even if they don't totally agree with a final decision, people are far more likely to support the result if they've been a respected part of the process by which it came about. Not only do they want to "see the research," they expect to be active participants. To have had a voice in the collection of data and of the factors that inform decision-making helps make it relevant to themselves, their work, and their support of the institution. Therefore it falls to conscious leadership to embrace this dynamic and include the membership or workforce body in the process such that they actually feel and know that inclusion.

Especially in a non-profit, the leader or leadership body is no longer the de facto decision maker. Rather, they are the decision manager, the decision shepherd, with inherent responsibility to hear from all sectors, appreciate all points of view, and include lots of people in the process toward developing policies and procedures—all before anything is announced or implemented. People need to feel heard in order to fully accept such decisions.

In the realm of short-term projects and programs in the creative industries (and some of the major grassroots NGOs), the best leaders and directors have long embraced the practice of listening to their teams as they explore options, standards, and policies. The fact is that this is now how all organizations need to function. Boards and leaders who believe that they know what is best for an organization without practical inclusion of the member-stakeholders of that organization are deluding themselves and short-changing the organization. Paternalism rears its outdated head.

Members want a voice, an actual voice, and an effective forum for that voice. The fact is that the strongest, most effective leaders do not believe that it is incumbent on them to have the answers. A good leader knows how to go about finding the answer, and, above all, is always willing to discover that they might not yet have arrived at the answer at any given moment. One needn't be right to get to the right answer…or any of the possible right answers.

The acceptance of that possibility—the management of membership bodies grounded in the acceptance of that philosophy—is what will empower the most effective leaders now and into the coming decades.

Wait! What? It has a toothpick?

Can one covet what one already has?

My Swiss Army Knife. I was in Boy Scouts, hiking and camping in the mountains of Oregon when I was given mine. For boys of a certain era, I believe, the possession of such a wonder was almost a rite of passage, a coming of age, the precursor to Mountain Manhood. Owning one made one cool…and able to accomplish anything.

I could whittle with the best, open things, pry things, cut kindling or meat or rope. I could do it all and was sure to carry this instrument with me at all times. Be Prepared, as the motto reminds us.

One evening over a campfire with a group of guys, as we cooked and ate our burgers, all with our Swiss Army

Knives attached to our belts, one of the guys got some gristle stuck between his teeth.

"Anyone got a toothpick…" he asked. Two of us looked uselessly at each other, thinking "Who packs tooth-picks for a camping trip?"

The fourth guy reached for his SAK, pulled out the toothpick and silently, smugly, handed it to him.

"Wait! WHAT? Yours has a toothpick!!?"

"YOURS have toothpicks…" he quietly said.

Oh.

Who knew?!

The lesson is that one ought never to assume they know everything about anything, no matter how familiar one is with that thing…or how familiar one believes they are with the thing.

Working with people, whether on a creative or produc-tion team—or anywhere else for that matter—it's easy to assume (Exploration of Assumption!) one knows everything relevant about the members of the team or of those whom one is directing. This is never so. People can almost always surprise us with another layer of creativity, another applicable experience from the past to apply to today's problem, or a deeper understanding of some thing that can miraculously expand horizons or enrich an experience.

Keep asking questions, keep minds open; as a proj-ect unfolds through its process, see to it that the atmosphere is open for contribution, innovation, and exploration of possibility outside one's own experience, vast or otherwise. Likewise, being familiar with or knowing someone else's body of work can make one an expert in what that person has done, but not an expert on that person or what they can do.

Be open, expect surprises, seek them out. I speak from show and experience production. I'll wager, though, that this dynamic applies in almost any business or academic context. You've worked with scores of designers, legions of creatives, producers, and technicians. They're all different...and they can each surprise you.

I'm just saying that simply because someone has "Art Director" on their business card, that individual may or may not work as other art directors work. Not all creative directors live in a cloud of their own reality (though, some...) and not all producers are...well, you know.

It's a good rule of thumb to approach afresh each person on the team, each time, to see what's new, what characteristics may have evolved since last contact, and what amazing and valuable properties may have been there all along without your awareness.

Keep exploring, remain ready to learn at all times and keep people around you who can surprise you with what they can do and how they can inspire you. I have just recently been newly inspired by people I had inadvertently misevaluated based on my experience of them. I offer, too, we should guard against forgetting that people evolve just as we do—exploring, discovering, learning, and growing.

Don't be the last one to know about the toothpick.

Explore.

9

**Responsibilities
of a Producer**

Years ago during a production meeting with one of my university clients, one of the higher-ranking well-respected, remarkably intelligent members of the oversight committee offered, shall we say, a rather unorthodox production idea. This individual had no background in theatre or show production. Everyone at the table looked over to the production manager as he considered our official response...

"You know," he said after a moment. "There are a lot of bad ideas...better than that!"

The group cracked up, and the point was made.

That point is that the customer is most definitely not always right, especially in show, theatrical, and experience production.

This is a nuanced balance, a delicate path one must walk. On the one hand, the client has contracted or engaged the producer to deliver a property or concept, to realize a vision. Often it's the vision of the client, sometimes one in which the client has a financial investment. Either way, the client is paying the producer to deliver what is wanted.

But who is the arbiter of what is wanted?

The hard truth is that the client isn't always (and by that, I mean rarely) the best judge of how to realize a given vision or concept. If that were the case the client would be the producer. The producer is paid and responsible for ensuring that the project actually happens, adheres to the budget, and gives the audience what the client wants them to get, to appreciate.

Let's step back for a minute and lay out some of the

Creative Catalyst

major, different kinds of producers. (None of these definitions are ironclad or static; the job descriptions tend to be a little flexible, depending on the project and who has the money.)

EXECUTIVE PRODUCER: This is who oversees the entire project, though sometimes this person is simply the one with the money.

PRODUCER: The one who knows how to put all the pieces together. They protect the director and the creatives from the money people and other realities while developing the vision.

MANAGING PRODUCER: This person is all about the nuts and bolts, scheduling, and budgets, and not so much about the content or look of the show itself.

CREATIVE PRODUCER: Often collaborates with the director or even handles some of the directing, handing off the logistical management details to a production manager or co-producer.

Sometimes actors are given producer credit as a perk, which can enhance the percentage of the money the film makes. And then there often might be the "carnal" producer: the boyfriend or girlfriend of the executive producer, another producer, or star of the show who wants a credit and something to do. There are other varieties of producers, but these are the typical ones.

Now, that being said, seldom does anyone wear just one of those hats. More often than not responsibilities are juxtaposed, distributed, and apportioned in different ways for different projects, depending on who brought in the property, who owns the theatre, who was there first, and so on. Ultimately, though, no matter how these positions and titles are crafted, there's a mysterious realm of creative realization and protection that lies between the producer and director. It is between these two that the nurturing and evolution of the audience experience lies.

Audience (and client) expectation is limited by what they know is possible. It is our job, our responsibility, as creators of experience to exceed audience expectation through what we know is possible, what we know is right, what we know will work best. Our job is to protect what the client wants the audience response to be, not accede to every suggestion, edit, or demand of the client at the risk of the actual experience.

This is where it can get dicey.

In most of my work, I generally act as Director of Concept Ideation, Creative Producer, or Creative Director, then often do the directing or collaborate with a specialized director for unique media or contexts. Sometimes I am fortunate to partner with a producer who can support the creative concept and process, deliver the production, while also protecting the logistical and budget details.

Here's the nuance within all of this. While what the client wants is of paramount importance, the expertise of the producer and creatives should supersede any contributions (suggestions, demands, etc) from the client that are detrimental to the realization of the vision. This, as one might imagine, is where diplomacy enters the picture.

While "there are a lot of bad ideas...better than that..." may not be the most diplomatic of responses, there are other ways of conveying and convincing a client to relinquish their opinions. While each client-suggested idea or approach may well sound fantastic as stand-alone concepts or components, very often the overall effect of acceding to client demands can result in a production that is disjointed, too long, suffers from depletion of energy, or simply fails to maintain a connection and realize the original vision. Or it's just bad.

As producer or director we are integrity-bound to stand up for the concept, trusting that we are there to protect that very thing.

I once worked with a producer who could not say "no" to the client. Ever. The result from him acquiescing to successive increments of two, three, and four minutes was a two-and-a-half-hour show that got extended nearly an hour.

An entire hour, all because of the adjustments and additions the client wanted. When the show was over and the reviews were in, the universal complaint was the exhausting length of the show. The client was angry at how the show was received and blamed the producer.

I believe the producer must hold the line with the client.

Do what you know is right

I learned this lesson years ago when producing and directing my first huge, international stadium spectacle: Closing Ceremonies for the Gay Games at Yankee Stadium in June of 1994. With 12,000 athletes from 60 countries in a stadium of 50,000, this was the most internationally visible of my productions to date, one of my largest audiences, and of massive importance to the Games movement.

The responsibility was great; the potential affect on my own career not negligible.

After six or seven months of blissfully working with my team in an unobstructed vacuum, collaborating with the creative and production teams to build a wonderful show arc and spectacle experience, the "committee" began to insert themselves into the process, second-guessing decisions that had long been made.

Things got tense; there were challenges. Much was riding on this spectacle for all of us. As the pressure increased, I spent several dark nights of the soul, examining my position(s) and assessing the spiritual costs, experiential risks, and professional exposure of holding the line on what I knew would play best versus acquiescing to the pressure from the committee.

The risk was high. A failure could be monumentally destructive, personally and professionally.

I finally came to this decision: were I to accede to the pressure and make changes I believed were ill-advised and the show were to bomb, I would have nothing but a failure to my name. However, were I to hold the line and stick to the vision, keep my integrity with respect to what I believed in my heart of hearts was the right thing...and the show were to bomb, then I would know, at least, that I had been wrong.

I decided that I'd prefer to at least risk coming to learn that I was wrong than to make changes in which I didn't believe. I would be happy with the lesson, were I to fail. That decision has served me for nearly two decades and gave me confidence in my own judgment during a rough time.

Which is not to say that I am not a good deal more dip- lomatic these days than I may have been at that time. What I know is that I must believe in what I am doing. I must keep clear sight on the vision, or I cannot do it. This does not mean the original vision cannot evolve; it virtually always does, often becoming something quite different and just as often far better.

Trust yourself, collaborate and communicate, and stay true to what you know. That, at least, is my advice.

Oh, and the show was a hit.

Respect your team

Pay the crew.

As producers, let's resolve to always pay our people on time.

So often I see the effects of sluggish or sloppy payment processes on the life of the freelancer, whether they are tech, production, artist, or other. Terms such as "net 30," "net 60," statements like "…we pay all our invoices quarterly…" are virtually incomprehensible, generally irrelevant, and always frustrating to the talent one hires.

Further, these people work for you, not your client. It is irrelevant to them whether or not you yourself have been paid for the work or show. YOU owe the money to the team, not your client.

Respect that.

So many people are uncomfortable around money and their own financial situations. Asking for money can feel deeply demeaning to most people. Be sensitive to this and find ways to avoid that doubt and discomfort that are far too often concomitant with working as a freelance artist or consultant.

It's not so difficult.

When a production is mine, one of my favorite moments is when I am able to circulate through the team during warm up or pre-rehearsal, quietly handing out checks face-to-face and hand-to-hand with thanks for all the hard work that's been put in. Paying in this manner shows tangible respect and helps cement the bond of trust between you, your talent, and tech.

They enter the stage happier, upbeat, and energetic and are able to leave the production—physically and mentally—confident and complete, with no doubts as to where and when they'll be paid.

This is big stuff.

Early money is like yeast; it will grow your reputation among peers and performers and grow your credibility with vendors and resources. You'll achieve greater results with these stronger relationships.

I have worked with a company in the UAE unlike any other in this respect. On the first or second day of my first collaboration with them in 2011, the accountants called me in and handed me the contract-specified per diem for the entire contract up front, in cash. No receipts necessary, no waiting, no outlay of my own funds. I could buy groceries or restaurant meals and pay for gasoline or taxis with no "approval" process. This made it so easy and showed me and the other consultants that we were supported by the company in getting done what we were brought over to get done.

On the last day of the contract, once again we were called into the accounting office, handed a check, and sent to the bank on the first floor to cash it before leaving for the airport. Clean and neat, respectful and easy. I've seen this company send a driver two hours to another city to offer performers their pay in cash; working during banking hours, away from their home cities and banks, make it difficult to deal with checks. This is a great policy and makes people feel appreciated in a fundamental and security-encouraging way.

Depending on what part of the world in which one is working, and the tech level of a given client, of course, the ideal way to be paid is wire transfer to one's bank. These days it's always a good idea to include wire transfer information on the invoice. Always make it as easy as possible to give you money!

It does take the producer (you...us) planning, advance conversations, and familiarization with the process and logistics of the financial people. You'll probably have to deal with some invoice-gathering at a really busy time, but it will yield a healthy cornucopia of positive results.

Feed the crew

Seriously, feed your darn crew.

The way to a person's best work is paved with taste buds and gastrointestinal comfort. You probably already know this. You must know this. But I think some don't, so I'm going to say it.

Decades ago, when producing press conferences for national and local political campaigns, and upon discovering that the press corps often had to be at their desks by 8am, I would hold press conferences at 8:30am and always provide donuts and coffee. That way they could be late to work, as they'd want to be in position before the conference began and get free breakfast.

Packed, every time.

Over twenty years in production I learned early on that the crew must be fed...and always a real meal.

This is not rocket science, but when I encounter a producer, director, project manager, client, or events person who begrudges or in any way resists the idea of feeding the crew, I am repeatedly stunned at their shortsightedness. And yes—I judge.

Seeing that the crew is fed is not about union rules and contracts; it's about building a team and infusing the qualities of collegiality and respect. A happy, well-fed crew knows they are appreciated and respected and will likely go the distance—above and beyond—when the situation calls for it. And in live show work you can pretty much count on the situation calling for it.

When a crew is treated as an expense, with marginal

craft service and meals and contractual boxes to be ticked in order to comply, one can expect that is how one's job or production will be treated. With such an attitude underlying the production, a crew can then be expected to do only what they are contracted to do and nothing more. Professionally professional, certainly, but a great show depends on that relationship being personally professional.

Communicating the importance of feeding the production crew is often one of the first "come to Jesus" conversations I find myself having with a new client… and sometimes with a regular one.

Sometimes those who may never really worry about food on the table fail to perceive its importance to those who live closer to the line. This also pertains to paying cast and crew at the close of the show so they depart with the deal complete and needn't worry about when they'll be paid.

A few years ago, on site with a colleague, she was grousing about the concern being expressed by her crew heads over the quality of the breakfasts that were being supplied. Skinny, aluminum-wrapped breakfast burritos seemed fine to her. "Why do they make such a big deal about breakfast?"

"Are you kidding? Seriously. Why buy a Ferrari and put unleaded fuel in it? You have a great crew; keep 'em happy and in top form. Scrambled eggs, biscuits, butter (not cold; it should be spreadable on arrival), jam, potatoes, and bacon…lots of bacon"—except in the Middle East—"and you'll have one of the smoothest-running shows you've ever had. Trust me."

Plus, your crew will be inclined to show up early for a good breakfast and be ready to go at call-time.

The Ferrari metaphor resonated; she upped the quality of breakfasts and the show production experience definitely cranked up several notches.

Your crew are the most important people you want committed to yourself as producer and to the vision of the experience or show you're all striving to deliver. The crew should know that the producer or director knows they are dependent on them and that genuine respect underscores the relationship. When that is known and appreciated, the crew are all about supporting the show and the vision.

The rewards for this commitment will become increasingly evident and valuable as crew members begin coming up with creative solutions to problems the producer may not yet have seen coming. They take ownership of the show at a more fundamental, personal level and treat the responsibilities under their purview with that much more acuity and concern for quality.

It's a human trait.

There existed an even greater dichotomy to be discovered during my years in Dubai. The caste distinction between levels of the production crew is even more pronounced in that part of the world, most especially between the (generally Western or First World) professional, creative, and technical individuals and the Third World labor class brought in to do the actual building.

Early on in my experience, it took much insistent negotiation with a client to obtain even a simple table of water bottles and bananas placed under a canopy, specifically for the laborers on a show or project. It also took a little friendly education to convince the laborers that there were no negative consequences for helping themselves to the table whenever they were thirsty or had a pang of hunger.

The smile and laughter quotient among the laborers tended to rise...and I'll tell you, experiencing all those guys smiling and quietly speaking or signaling a greeting as they passed rather than having them silently avert their eyes from "sir" is transformational and spiritually empowering.

Feed your crews.

Don't yell at the crew

A producer never yells at or belittles a crew or crew member—especially in public. ALL public communication must remain respectful and, when there is a problem, the wise, experienced producer collaborates with the crew or crew member to address it and come up with the best solution to the problem. Any upbraiding, criticism, or firing is always done in private. Always.

A producer who shouts at a crew sows seeds of disrespect and mistrust, conveying a sense of ownership that is at cross-purposes to the spirit of show and project crew culture. The best work comes through respect.

Shouting and berating is amateur.

Such a producer will have a hard time engendering loyalty and finding crew colleagues willing to join the next project.

Value their time

It is critical to be sensitive to the natures and processes of your creatives. Conversely, it can turn out to be quite expensive to dismiss or eschew this respectful sensitivity.

How not to do it: not so long ago I had the misfortune to participate in a "creative overview & notes" meeting on a production of great magnitude. It turned out to offer a great example of how not to treat one's creatives.

The purpose of the meeting was to give meticulous direction to the development of the visual creative to a team of consultants four time zones away via Zoom. To participate in this meeting, those creatives had to be up and running before the sun. Anyone who knows and has worked with brilliance knows that artists can tend to be late risers. Despite that, the creative director had called this meeting for 9:00am local time.

We and the creative director were gathered in the conference room for a prep meeting on the project, scheduled to end and flow into the creative briefing. But this previous meeting began to run overtime. Several reminders that we had these other men waiting in their studio for us to connect went unacknowledged by the creative director for a full forty minutes—at which time he announced that he needed a cigarette. He got up and left the room with a few other members of the executive team to have a smoke.

Twenty minutes later, a full hour past the scheduled time, the CD returned and the meeting finally commenced. One could readily see on the faces of the remote artists their ire at being treated so dismissively.

This early interaction affected pretty much all future interaction between this company and the artists, both electronically and in face-to-face meetings...and definitely in the quality of the finished product.

This made for an exceptionally expensive hour. Not only in the practical costs of paying for creative consulting time that went completely unused, but the negative effects of this dismissive and thoughtless act were felt throughout the rest of the production. Treatment such as this can (and in this instance, most certainly did) color the tone of an entire production and have far-reaching costs well beyond the immediate and tangible.

Such disrespectful disregard for the time, process, and work of one's team members affects not only the working relationship but also the actual product. Irrespective of one's commitment to professionalism, when one is treated poorly it will ultimately affect the nuance of the work and the relationships among the collaborators, especially when it comes to "crunch time." Ultimately, it affects resilience, responsiveness, and—most critically—creativity.

It is a wise discipline to develop and hone, to remember you are dealing with people who have lives and sched-ules of their own. We do not own them; they are not our property for pulling from a virtual shelf to use at will.

Respect your team. Show it.

Protect your team

Protect your creatives.

Protect your creative relationships.

Protect your product and production.

You're the producer, so produce. Your job is to protect the creative(s) from the barrages of reality as concept and vision evolve and develop into experience. Your job is to protect the budget from the wild and expensive ideas of your creatives when approaches less grand might be more effectively evocative. In the absence of a creative director, your job is to wear both hats and to exhibit and earn respect for and from both camps, ultimately creating a united team out of the technical production side and the creative development and interpretation side.

Take credit for recruiting the right people. Give credit freely and unhesitatingly to those who really do the work. The more you give credit and acknowledge source and inspiration, the better you look and the stronger your relationships will be with the teams you build. Become known for the teams you build and what they create.

Do not manage by committee. Just don't.

Your job as fulcrum for the production, as protector of creative and budget, and as shepherd of the show is to protect all processes. This is how you will protect your budget and your relationships as you work to achieve and present the best possible experience.

One point of contact

Your job is to filter the input and share what is appropriate with your creative, production, or technical professionals. You are the one point of contact with the world outside the production. Your duty is to protect that relationship at all costs.

You'll discover two distinct benefits to this process:

Your team will trust and appreciate you, resulting in a more candid "in-house" give-and-take and sharing of ideas as concepts and approaches evolve. You can share an idea you've gleaned from another source and get candid feedback from your creatives without risking offense to your external source. You can then, with integrity, make informed decisions in the context of your project and vision and continue to massage your project in line with that understanding and appreciation.

You protect the clarity of the vision. Remember, irrespective of the esteem in which you may hold your mentors and advisors, their advice is based on limited exposure to your concept and approach. Listen fully, consider thoroughly, but only adopt and share what truly makes sense. You must be the filtering arbiter, period.

Above all, do not allow "committees" of people to offer input to your project to anyone but yourself. And by committee, I mean anyone but you. There are few ways more sure to derail a relationship or project than allowing direct input from more than one person. The net effect is nearly always deleterious to your project, diluting potential potency, and will definitely undermine your working relationships within the team. Do not unleash these people on your team.

Trust, once broken, can never be fully restored.

As producer and leader of the team, you set the tone and establish the standards for your team. It is your example by which members of your team should be inspired and offer themselves measure. Your integrity must be sacrosanct; the respect with which you treat others should be unshakeable, your communications clear and complete, your leadership inspirational and enlightening.

This really isn't difficult, if the commitment is within you. That and a little zen discipline and you're there.

Be accountable

Responsibility for anything that goes wrong with the production is on your shoulders. This means that you jump up and acknowledge responsibility for anything that goes wrong or falls short without a second thought. Never let an employee take the fall. Not publicly, in any case.

Conversely, anything that goes uniquely or impressively right with the production is an opportunity for you to publicly acknowledge the professionals on your team who are directly responsible for what stood out. 'Tis a good rule of thumb to simply never take credit. Always find someone to credit, or simply credit your team.

Without that team you're just a big good-looking bundle of good ideas (and maybe not even all that good, without the collaboration of the gang that makes it great).

Creative Catalyst

Be responsible

Words are one thing; actions quite another. A solid leader pays attention to the little things that might be overlooked or fall between the cracks in a large bureaucracy.

This does not mean be a micromanager.

What it means is that, as a production ramps up and the work is getting done, the one in charge must be sure the team is being supported by the infrastructure. Payments are made on time, insurance is carried and covered, breaks are taken, and people are fed. That craft services has carbs, protein, and abundant amounts of chocolate and sugar.

In our world, it is not unusual for a show to close or a project to wrap with a vendor or freelancer not yet paid. It should be unusual but it isn't, unfortunately. Sometimes things move fast, invoices get lost, payment is assured and assumed but not actually delivered. Many such things can result in that one payment not happening. When this happens, the one who was in charge remains responsible for the clearing of accounts. The producer or director may be on to another project, as may the individual or vendor who is still owed money.

But being separated from the project is irrelevant; it remains our responsibility see to it that that artist or technician is paid, especially if we are ever going to want work from that person in the future.

Remain approachable. Work to be approachable—watch out for seeming "too busy" to be interrupted.

Each such interruption likely bears the potential for some learning, some evolution, some exchange of ideas, or even the sharing of information that can perhaps save time or money down the line. Guard against dismissiveness and discount no one.

Vest your people with responsibility and let them know you mean it.

This takes discipline for the Type A personality, but if you really want to build a dependable and ultimately reputable team, then delegate…and mean it.

I launch virtually any production with a few regular conversations, one of which is the stressing of the fact that, on my teams, no one will be penalized for making a mistake, miscalculation, or misjudgment. Penalty is levied when that mistake is hidden or kept secret. The moment a team member sees that what is intended may not happen as envisioned—that's the moment to raise the flag.

When someone makes a mistake, that person is probably the one best qualified to devise and implement a solution. Ergo, when someone comes to me with a mistake, my first response (after the "oops," "omg," or "holy crap!") is usually, "well, what would you suggest we do?" And we figure it out together.

This teaches practical skills and problem-solving and is a compelling and resonant example of the trust you are placing in your team. This makes what you have been saying tangible and makes you trustworthy to them. And, pertinent to what I was saying earlier, should one of the team come under fire for a real or perceived error, the immediate response of the producer is to

Creative Catalyst

stand by his team and take any heat, resolving direct responsibility issues offline and in private.

If your team knows you will stand by them, they will go the extra mile for you.

They will push the envelope and take considered (and some not-so-considered) risks in the pursuit of higher standards of storytelling and production.

I want to underscore the responsibilities of the producer with a comment from Ben Tripp, brilliant artist and author:

The one-point-of-contact thing really is critical. A couple of other things that happen with diffuse communication:

Conflicting critiques—a couple of executives may have directly contradictory opinions. They deliver their reactions independently and expect results. This leads to creatives acting as liaisons, taking sides, or believing the process had broken down (which it has). In addition, specialists can create difficulties by delivering their criteria without regard for the rest of the show. I was once on an entertainment project in which the PM gave equal voice to a guy way upstream whose central role was leasing real estate. So the entire design ended up geared to making it really easy to swap out retail tenants.

You need communication to flow through the point man—the filter.

—https://www.bentripp.info

Time and again I see weak producers taking opinions from far too many others, not trusting their professional instincts enough to take responsibility for the result. Go out on a limb, dammit, and stand behind your beliefs, your instincts, what you trust in your heart.

Remember, you are vested with the result, with realizing the vision, with knowing how best to manifest the idea. You cave and it bombs, you'll be blamed. At least be able to "own" your bombs...do that, and you'll have far fewer, if any, of them.

Future planning

A good leader, a responsible leader, plans for what happens after they are gone.

Never assume longevity. A good leader remains proactively aware that one's tenure on any project or in any company will always come to a close. Usually you know it's coming, but sometimes it can sneak up disastrously ill-timed.

One of the key—if not crucial—responsibilities of leadership is preparing for one's untimely departure. Focused foresight and planning are integral parts of upholding one's responsibility as leader. Don't be responsible for leaving teams, projects, and companies rudderless.

This is why many companies restrict the number of executives that can travel together; the risk of losing vast amounts of institutional and operational knowledge is simply too great. However, it is not only large companies that call for the planning of someone's exit. The fact is that any team needs to be prepared with succession plans for principal losses, most especially that of the leader.

How to prepare one's team? Simple stuff!

Share information

We've talked about the value of sharing information
and how it empowers your team and individual investment in the project or goal. Implemented from the start
and maintained on a continuous basis, the ongoing
sharing of information as a project evolves is key to
the successful stepping up of a temporary surrogate or
permanent replacement.

Keep your team informed

Involve the team in the decision-making process.
Seeking input and informed opinion prepares the
entire body for the departure of any one individual.
Maintaining engagement of all your team members
ramps up personal investment in the project or company and tends to result in a far tighter and more
responsive team—and exponentially better result.

When it's the leader who is leaving, the confidence and
value of the person stepping into their shoes—knowing
the how's and why's of previous decisions and courses
of action—cannot be overstated. Shared knowledge is
power. Secrets undermine.

Don't risk a departure or absence that leaves your
team(s) adrift; this is a fundamental betrayal of the
trust placed in leadership. Plan for departure from the
first day; don't leave it to the last minute as there may
not be a "last minute" to build and activate a plan.

Share relationships

Even if one is the primary point of contact with the client or executive on the job, even if one is the virtual fulcrum for the program, plan, or operation, the simple practice of including one or two select members of the team to participate or at least sit in on meetings reaps rewards in numerous ways:

1. Knowledge of nuance.
2. Exposure and credibility as competent leaders in and of themselves—to the client, but also to themselves and their team members.
3. Status as empowered lieutenants who can be deployed to handle situations when the leader is occupied.
4. Generates trust in the entire team by the client as well as mutual trust within the team in stepping up and moving forward when any member departs.

Not doing this undermines everything. Information unshared is, again, a virtual land mine. A good leader gives exposure, credibility, and respect to one's teammates or lieutenants. This brings fresh perspective into meetings and conversations and will foster respect and authority for these individuals who may need to stand in for the leader at any time. These very people, in the leader's absence, will need to be clear on the history of the relationship or project to be able to operate with ease and comfort in your stead and to be conversant in the evolution of the project and relationship—to deliver the desired outcome.

Creative Catalyst

Be aware of who is on the team

Especially in an industry where freelancers and consultants move from project to project, company to
company, even country to country year after year,
guard against viewing individual members as defined
by the job done or task being filled at the moment. In
many parts of the world, management tends to view
individuals merely as the jobs they are performing, with
no thought or curiosity as to what resource or potential
these individuals might represent. Not only is this dismissive to the body of work, skills, and talents likely represented by the individuals on the teams, it is a hugely
expensive shortsightedness on the part of leadership.

Though respect for a staffing plan may be honorable,
strict adherence to it may be foolhardy. As projects
evolve and the numerous unforeseen obstacles and
opportunities arise, knowledge of the background,
experience, and potential on the team can possibly
solve the issue in moments or hours, rather than days,
weeks, and months.

Don't assume, don't pigeonhole.

Share your knowledge

Mentor. Teach. Share. Ask. Involve.

This does not mean lecture, pontificate, order, and
berate. Rather, it means open up and be willing to learn
at every juncture, throughout the process of the work.
The time and money saved, the powerful increase in
morale, the increased productivity and responsiveness of one's team, and the possibility of spectacular

realization of goal that's well above and beyond the original vision is worth it.

One of my favorite anecdotes from my own history is the time two decades ago when my production team was wrestling with a dilemma with an imminent show. This was a spectacle with over 12,000 participants in an iconic structure in New York City. Very public, very big, only one shot at success. These were not "closed" meetings, as I believe anyone who wants to know how things are going should be welcome. One never knows.

From the back of the room, during a pensive lull in our conversation, came the voice of one of the crusty old "union guys," a driver on the project. "Well," he says, "back in 1975 we had the same problem with [name of show and diva redacted!]. What WE did was…" and he gave us our solution.

One never knows.

Trust your people.

Know your people.

Shine a light on your assets.

New clients may come to you or your company based on your reputation. They will stay with you and, more importantly, return to you based on the experience they had working with you. That means it will be the personal experience with the people on your team that will bring them back.

Business is personal. We've said it before, and it cannot be overstated.

Knowing this, the wisest approach to the development of client relationships is keeping in mind the fact that longevity with the client will be a direct result of the work delivered and the people delivering that work.

So, set them up to succeed.

Show off your people. Give your client the opportunity to know who and why each person is on your team, to be impressed at the wealth of skill, talent, and experience you have accumulated and made available to your clients. Don't hide them behind a screen of corporate anonymity; conversely, don't allow the client to give direction to your team. Be sure your people know to direct the client to see you about any instructions they attempt to give in situ. Your team will be forever grateful—as will your accountant.

When we bring a new talent onto a team, we take care and effort to introduce that person to the rest of the team along with the traits, talents, and accomplishments that brought that person on board.

Rather than a simple, "This is Tom, our new Art Director…" we augment that introduction with "You gotta spend time with this guy; he's done amazing stuff. He publishes his own cartoon strip, writes and performs music, surfs like a demon, and has cured cancer, twice! Get to know him and welcome him to our team."

This serves two primary purposes:

1. This gives the rest of the team a context within which to get to know the new person, to ask questions and discover mutual interests. In other words, to launch the bonding…it makes this new individual more of a person from the start.

2. This also serves to render the rest of the team conversant in the qualifications of that individual, what unique things that person brings to the table to augment the team.

Each team member should be able to authentically and enthusiastically give testimony as to the uniqueness of each of the rest of the team.

Which brings us to why this same practice is something we ought do when bringing or sending a team into a project or client.

Sending or bringing along a team under the banner of your company is one thing; it's impressive at the outset, but with an effect that ultimately dissipates and even disappears if your people aren't introduced as highly valuable in their own right. Blow your clients away at the quality of the team you have gathered for this project; impress them at your acumen for finding and hiring good people and let your client know what makes each so fantastic.

These are the people who, working with you, for you, or under your banner, make you look good. Capitalize on that.

Rather than "This is Sheila, the Project Coordinator for your project…" try instead, "Client, meet Sheila."

Creative Catalyst

She has a few years of producing live television under her belt, has worked in China and Australia and kicked some ass in the process. She is one of the most organized people I've ever found and we're lucky to have her. She'll be Project Coordinator on your project…at least, until we promote her…"

This approach will give your client more confidence in work, opinion, or suggestion that comes from Sheila. It will build trust in her and in your entire team. This approach will unfailingly communicate to your team that they are trusted.

Further, as work is delivered, as components and projects come online, credit those who actually do the work. Let your client know who wrote the script, who drew the schematic, who created the amazing artwork, who discovered that a wrong bolt was specified for the rocket launcher. Credit your people and you will look even better. But, tuck that individual contribution behind the impersonal banner of the company in some digest or unattributed document and nobody gains… and the opportunity is missed for acknowledgment, morale boosting, and a deepening of the personal relationship.

If you present and treat your teams as no more than a roster of titles, they will be seen as no more than that—virtually interchangeable. Give them context, give them credibility, empower them to act in your stead when you are not available, and this will only grow your reputation for astuteness and clarity.

Give credit where it's due

Put your people in the spotlight as they create or deliver exceptional work.

Everyone already knows you are The One, the creative visionary, the impresario producer. That you drive the idea or concept and the team. That you are in charge. The world already knows that. My suggestion is to be relaxed and secure in your position and give all the credit to those who deliver for you.

When someone approaches you after seeing your show or experiencing the thing you made and says, "Oh, Kile"—if, in fact, your name is Kile—"that was amazing! I still can't get over the moment when <whatever impressed them> happened. I will remember that for the rest of my life! THANK YOU!" That is your opportunity to publicly and graciously point to and acknowledge the person or team that made that one component happen for you, throwing attention and accolade their way.

"You know who did that? That was David, John, and Melissa; they're right over there. I'd appreciate it if you'd go over and tell them what you just told me. In fact, let me introduce you..."

...or some practical form of immediate acknowledgment:

- Share their contact information.
- Cite their work when interviewed.
- Spontaneously recommend them when the subject of their craft comes up amongst peers and colleagues.

Push and promote those who have delivered for you; it only makes you look generous and supportive and ego free...and we know you are at least two of those things.

The rewards and benefits of such a stance are legion. I can attest to the good feeling of handing off compliments, the power of the trust that is built and grows when your team knows you respect and appreciate them. The security that exists and builds in knowing that these professionals will likely jump with alacrity at the chance to work again with someone who treats them fairly and readily shares the glory.

These are your relationships to protect

Developing and maintaining a reputation for being committed to the well-being and professional treatment of those who work under you will ultimately give you a great reputation for respecting your people. It will also result in those people trusting you, implicitly, and returning to you in the future.

Anecdotally, this is how it has played out for me.

I do work in theme parks, for non-profits and NGOs, and for corporations. When I have a good budget and a well-paying gig, I pay my teams accordingly...and always on time. The men and women who have worked for me in stadiums, theatres, urban malls, and ballrooms have never been in doubt about the respect (and often awe) in which I hold and treat them. We get great results, virtually every time.

At other times, when I have accepted a project for a weakly-funded charity or smaller entity, I can reach out to these same people, sharing with them the fact that "There's no money in this one...," and they remain highly likely to jump onboard and join me on the project because:

- They know that they will be treated with respect.
- They will be paid on time, no matter how minuscule the payment.
- They will be asked to collaborate on something emotionally engaging and likely quite fulfilling to them, personally and professionally.
- They will very likely get to see me cry, more than once, as the experience unfolds...and chances are they will also be moved.

Not a bad reputation to have. Not a bad offer to make. Good practice for work and life.

Following these guidelines will ensure power to attract good people to do good work. It is working in this way that will offer the reputation for edge, for creativity, for creating healthy, collaborative, and fun environments that yield compelling experiences. It will make your teams attractive to others, lessen the amount of coal in your stocking at Christmas, and lower the number of voodoo dolls made in your image.

10

Working With Your Team

M anaging creativity is, in and of itself, a creative process. The same input or feedback, depending on the point of view and motivation with which it is given, can serve either to evolve or impede the realization of a concept in development.

Team feedback

Certainly, the work needs to be examined with a critical eye. Step-by-step assessment of progress in the context of all possibilities must be made, feedback and direction given. How, however, that input is delivered can make all the difference in the final result and in the morale of the team. Team morale is, fundamentally, what drives productivity, creativity, loyalty, quality, and—make no mistake—future business.

In the words of Johnny Mercer, "Accentuate the positive, eliminate the negative..."

The same experienced eye can see and share feedback and direction in myriad ways, falling into two easy categories—positive and negative. That eye can look at facets in development on a project and see:

Something wrong, or...
    Something that can be evolved.

The terms and voice in which feedback is shared will make all the difference in what comes out the other side...what we get back.

Critique, given positively, nurtures good energy, supports open creativity and the flow of ideas, and paves

Creative Catalyst

the way for good work done well and quite likely done faster.

It all comes down to us, the managers, directors, producers, and so on and how we train ourselves to see things.

You have a choice.

When presented with concept, do you view it with the idea of seeing what is wrong with it, looking for problems and pointing them out, directing the solution with your own specifics from that point of view?

Or:

Do you first look for what is great about what you see, seeking to identify and embrace the creativity and inspiration behind it? And through that filter, does it offer opportunities for those who are doing the creating to resolve what you see, to evolve the concept over and around any obstacles?

Certainly, if something can be done better, it should be. That's the point of what we do. "A man's reach should exceed his grasp, or what's a Heaven for...?" (*Robert Browning, 1855*)

By seeking and inspiring solutions to possible problems we see from our creative team who are already responsible and invested, we can evolve what is already good within the project and the chaff will very likely fall away...simply through the process.

"No. Do it this way..." will result in exactly the opposite. Creativity will be squelched, inspiration doused, energy depleted, and your project becomes a job.

Tragic.

The power of positivity is incontrovertible. It takes as much discipline and self-control as any other important habit. The rewards for creating and working in such an environment are immeasurable.

Patience

Patience. It may be a virtue, but that doesn't make it all bad.

This has become one of my most valuable tools. That, combined with the realization and knowledge that there is always time for patience. Always.

Some years ago, there was a young man who worked at my side in Dubai. He was so well-suited to this work that within a year he was on his way to take a position in Abu Dhabi at a fantastic new destination waterpark. I was and still am proud of this man; he learned lessons rapidly, by necessity, and by rising to new challenges every day. Through these tests, as his self-awareness and confidence expanded, he grew into a man and producer who meets, exceeds, and sets new standards in expected levels of competence.

My last words of advice to him were, "Don't be the first person to speak at a meeting."

What do I mean by that?

The exercise of patience in any context, especially meetings. First, listen. Listen to everyone. Learn the lay of the land, discern how the subject on the table is perceived by and affects each individual in the room. As conversation and debate continue, the listener may find his own opinion or point of view changing and growing into a more comprehensive scope, incorporating points of view and appreciating ramifications as they reveal themselves through the discussion. When you finally say something, you can now incorporate all that has been expressed, possibly articulating the best course of action toward a most fully supportable and valuable result.

Eyebrows rise, words of acclamation are uttered —"Wow, you really nailed it...such clarity from one so young"—and the seeds of peer and superior respect are planted and nurtured. This, all because listening was happening and, along with that, learning.

This does not mean enter the room, knowing what one wants to say, and simply wait to say it. We've all been in conversations and arguments with others where it's obvious, as we are making a point, that our adversary is simply waiting for us to stop talking so they can rebut what they assume we are saying.

Instead, it means entering the room knowing one's point of view while also understanding there may be unseen assumptions in one's own point of view that can come to light in the ensuing conversation, affecting anything from nuance to critical component. Thus, exercising this patience allows the conversation to inform and evolve one's own position before that position is stated.

Not just for meetings

This patience thing applies far beyond the walls of the meeting room, however. It's applicable to virtually every step in the creative and production process and

applies no matter how much or how little time is at
one's disposal to create and deliver.

After the WaterWorld opening show I was being driven
to the airport by my producer, Adam, who mentioned
how much he had learned from me. Usually when someone says something like that I offer a heartfelt thanks,
appreciating that someone bothered to listen to me.
But this gent was one of the best producers with whom
I've worked; he was a brilliant man. So I asked him what,
in fact, he could possibly have learned from me. His
response was to cite my process over the extremely tight-
ly-scheduled rehearsal time in the run-up to the show.

What he was referencing was this:

1. The show was to be up and ready by
   10:00am on Saturday.

2. My directing partner would arrive Wednesday from London.

3. Thirty disparate acrobats and street performers were coming Wednesday night.

4. Blocking, rehearsal, costume fitting, and tech
   were all to take place on Thursday.

5. Rehearsals and dress rehearsal would happen Friday.

6. Show on Saturday. No extensions.

I might add that we HAD written a wonderful show for
the opening months before. A week before the show
was to open, the owner decided to change the time of
his party from 8pm to 2pm...thus our fabulous nighttime
plan of fiery waterfalls, giant synchronized pearl water

Creative Catalyst

ballet, and sparklers and fireworks were out the pro-verbial window. After an hour of grief, I contacted the agent in London and gave him the news. We explored a couple of ideas, then decided to just go ahead and bring down all the performers we'd already contracted and build the now-daytime show on the spot. And that's what we did.

So, on Wednesday evening I met with Steven Grindle to sync ourselves on the beats of the show. (Steven was also known as Dingle Fingle. This crazy creative descends from a long line of court jesters, minstrels, and magi-cians; he is virtual royalty and a legend, not only in his own mind but for anyone with whom he's worked.) We had not met prior to that evening, but we had corresponded with script ideas and possibilities and both came highly recommended by Mr. Proto. So we were inclined to expect good chemistry. We were not disappointed.

Still, one never knows what another might mean by virtually any word, term, or phrase. My "blue" might be cobalt while yours might be azure. So, even though we went gangbusters on the paper script we built, we really didn't yet know how the other man worked.

But we knew what we wanted to create.

On Thursday morning we gathered at the site, first touring the newly formed corps de fantasy through the park, then talking through the script before blocking artist movements for the show. Mind you, most of these performers had not previously worked together. This was not a corps until we all became such through these two days of rehearsals. Between the two of us, Steven speaks far better acrobat than I can even pretend. (Another rule of production: never pretend.) So, for most of Thursday I pretty much stood back—watching, listening, observing, supporting Steven, making suggestions, and keeping us as close to schedule as possible.

What I did not do is impose my vision on this group of performers who are skilled, talented, and creative in their own right, nor on Mr. Grindle, who works very differently than do I. My focus on Thursday was to learn how he works, learn who we had in our cast and how they fit or played together, and—in being passive and observant—communicating that I trusted Grindle and the corps to do their best work.

This is my process and is what Adam was referencing.

It is common for directors to step in, assert themselves, get all alpha on the project, and take the reins from the beginning. Though common, it's probably not always the best approach for fully realizing an evolved vision and obtaining maximum value drawn from each and every artist.

When a producer or director genuinely respects the unknown depths of talent in the individuals that make up a cast, and they communicate that trust by example, the wealth of creative collaboration is immeasurable. Our cast was brilliant beyond expectation, working together and offering suggestions as we built the show, and the result was far beyond what we might have hoped for during the limited two-day rehearsal period.

So on Thursday I trusted and learned...nudged a little when necessary...and kept working on where we wanted to take this show, writing and re-writing in my head. Friday, adding forty local performers to the mix, I took a partnership position in directing rehearsals, working through difficult or cumbersome scenes with Dingle and collaborating with him in making key decisions.

The two of us have very, very different management styles and the revelation was how great we could toss the ball from one to the other without conflict. An exciting experience of collaboration, it was pretty fantastic, challenging, and eminently rewarding.

Trust. Respect. Patience.

I would say that this was due in no small part to patience. Taking the time, no matter what, no matter how short the time seemed, to learn what lay before me, what tools were in our box, and to finesse a show out of this bounty of talent and energy. Which isn't to say that Dingle's trust and patience with me didn't contribute just as greatly to our mutual success as my own. Two professionals, up to their elbows in it.

"Don't be the first to speak at a meeting" applies across the board to any context in which you find yourself. Look and listen first, no matter how pressured you might feel to take action. Taking action without full knowledge will almost inevitably result in delay, difficulty, cost overruns, and wasted time. Take it up front; the investment pays off.

Sharing information

While I do appreciate the philosophy and fact that Information is power, what I take from that is that the more information people on my team possess, the more powerful the team becomes. So, I share.

Many a time will come when a manager, client, or executive will be encountered who considers information to have value only when they are in sole possession of it. To share information is perceived to subsume power. I say, not so much. There are people who withhold information until they think you need it...usually shortly after irrevocable and costly decisions have been made that would have been done differently had that information been made available from the start.

Thus my practice is generally to share as much as possible, when it's possible. Share with your team how you are making your decisions early on. Give them a sense of parameter, client idiosyncrasy, possible roadblocks, and eventualities that may materialize down the line; they will be more trusting of your judgment when the pace ramps up, decisions have to be made, and actions taken more quickly. They will be a team willing to trust as they've been trusted.

The added advantages to this are:

1. The way is paved for ad hoc delegation of responsibility. An informed assistant can make better on-the-spot decisions if they have the information.

2. When a situation arises that calls for rapid exploration of options and concomitant decision-making; the information-sharer is more likely to be surrounded with an informed team, capable of making recommendations from different perspectives, thus increasing the likelihood of the best possible solution being found and implemented.

Creative Catalyst

11

**Tools of
Production**

On the day of show, when a producer is seen running around, walkie-talkie against the ear while in heated discussions with crew or cast, putting out fires, sweating, and being extremely busy—one is likely witnessing a producer who is in way over their head.

A producer who knows the job and is good at it has resolved or circumvented all foreseeable problems. Teams have been built and briefed, tech is spec'd, riders are filled, and the script is familiar to the support players by day of show. On that day the competent producer awakens refreshed, confident, with everything in order—fully abreast of the status of all components of the production, having thought through the myriad possible negative eventualities and, if necessary, prepared to switch to Plan B...or C...or...

"Producers" who are swamped and busy on show days are the sort that give the actual good producers a bad name. A competent producer's time on show day is spent handholding the client and being available to make last-minute decisions for unforeseen eventualities. Show day should be calm.

All these "shoulds"...

Show day ought be about tiny tweaking of the production, making final adjustments, dealing with water main breaks and recalcitrant smoke alarms...not building the show.

No angst.

There are a few primary things among the hundreds on the original To Do list that continue to serve me and my productions extremely well in the run-up to a show.

The TimeLine

From the moment plans begin for a production of any magnitude, a single document is created to which only one person has editorial access and on which each and every single component and action of the production is included. If it's going to happen, it's on that document; if it is not on that document, it does not happen. I call this my "TimeLine." It includes all the components of a runsheet, production schedule, and script.

It works—fantastically.

This process is a lot of work, but creating the document ensures that I know the show top to bottom, every step of the way. By running production meetings with this document as driver, all hands-on principals are as versed in the entire show as anyone on the team. If something goes wrong, the closest person to the problem knows what's needed. Fully informed, the team is fully empowered.

From the very first decisions, every meeting is listed (along with where and when, who's attending, and who's responsible for seeing that the meeting actually happens), every site visit, every delivery, every parking slot, and load-in time. As the production develops the document grows and begins to reflect every call-time, every warning, every cue, and every speech or bit of script.

In my productions, whether I am creative producer or director, I generally build and maintain this document myself. If something changes, it only becomes official when it shows up in the TimeLine. If someone wants to change their script, that needs to be reflected on the

TimeLine (or the change will likely not show up on the TelePrompTer). This way I know what components are not showing up on deadline and who isn't delivering. I have a clear sense of timing, of how long the show runtime looks, how tight the schedule is, where there is play and where we are going to need to shave or cut something.

I was recently part of a production where the client arrived on show day with new scripts (in new typefaces) offering no indication of what had been changed and what had remained constant. No one knew the status of the script until the dress rehearsal, and even then the show was in flux up until the last minute. We pulled it off, but a central, respected and adhered-to document such as I use would have alleviated this dynamic.

Every addition or change needs to go through one person—the fulcrum—and is distributed as a PDF document.

Production meetings

In parallel with the development and maintenance of the TimeLine document is the full team production meeting. To me, this is obvious—a gimme. But I have been surprised at the number of times I witness producers who short circuit their own productions by dismissing the importance of this forum. Instead, they seem to hold information to themselves and dole out details on a "need-to-know" basis.

I'm the opposite. I believe that information is most valuable when shared.

Thoroughly communicating with all teams on a production is no substitute for getting everyone (and, by that, I mean EVERYONE) involved in the production in the same place at the same time to talk through the script, minute by minute. In my experience, these documents very often define moments and action down to the half- or quarter-minute. Not only does this give the team a compelling sense of timing and order of show, but it also makes clear the flow of activity for each individual component or person, from offstage arrival to onstage performance, and back again.

This exercise, conducted a few weeks prior to the show (and then again a day or two before) gives everyone from craft service to stage manager a very clear picture of what is to happen. Everyone then knows when, as well as where, everything and everyone else is to be at any given moment. This is very handy when something goes awry and a quick substitution is needed. Everyone knows who and what is where and can make informed, professional decisions or suggestions and substitu- tions on the fly, not depending on finding someone higher up to assess the situation.

A thoroughly-informed crew of professionals is invalu- able and will make the producer look damn good in some of the most difficult situations.

They can also save money for the production.

As different teams (electrical, technical, staging, lighting, props, whatever) share their load-in require- ments and logistical pieces of the puzzle, time and again I have witnessed spontaneous suggestions from contractors that make a positive difference. They could share truck space to save money for the pro- duction, adjust or trim load-in and load-out times, and coordinate all sorts of logistics. All because they were together in the same room. Usually, after the full talk-through of the script, the group splits into break-outs for at-the-moment problem solving.

This also makes for an exceptionally cohesive production team, which is darn handy at load-in, through the show, and during load-out.

Production crews very often get quite a chuckle at my TimeLines...and they also keep and save them, as these documents reflect the vision for the show and communicate, at an almost visceral level, the tightness with which the show must run. And it generally does run just that tight.

You never know. Listen.

Ten minutes of listening can save hours, days, thousands of dollars.

The other thing about listening—the magical thing—is the transformation of the group dynamic when it is practiced.

Here's a truth: When people feel authentically heard, they become far less likely to resist and far more likely to accept and embrace the results or outcome of a conversation or process. This means, on the other hand, that we must listen, authentically, until the statement or idea is out, communicated, and fully articulated. There can be no answer-building until the thought is fully expressed. A producer (or any leader) who does this will:

1. likely learn something new or see a new perspective, and

2. experience far less, if any, resistance to the final decision when it is made, even when it is not in alignment with the original arguments posed against it.

A professional crew will respect the fact that you listen and is likely to be more supportive of the project and deferential to the producer. Plan, plan, plan, and listen, listen, listen. Then make your best decision and move forward. Just don't forget your TimeLine!

Staff up!

Staff your talent. All of them.

Every principal in your show should have one person whom they can identify as their go-to, their font of knowledge, their responsible person. Never leave talent to their own devices for anything. To do so is more than just going against protocol and trying to avoid being perceived as careless, ignorant, or rude. It's simply the way one treats people.

Remember, often these people are not familiar with the venue, much less the town or the audience. Don't leave these people to fend for themselves, no matter how secure or self-possessed they may seem. Staff them. Especially for those who do charity work; don't unleash your talent into VIP receptions without a staff person at their side.

At. Their. Side.

Whether it's Eilish or Elton, LeBron or Lizzo, Gaga or Styles, provide them someone whom they can trust who will not be afraid to take them by the arm and say to the Krazy Glue throng around them, "I'm sorry, Miss Knowles is needed in the Press Room..." and protect them from having to fend for themselves.

This applies even when they arrive with their own people. In such cases, your wrangler becomes a resource and teammate to their people, though no less valuable. Don't overlook this—you will be respected and remembered for having handled this responsibility and professionally.

Assiduous. Complete. Respectful. Respected.

When writing scripts and shows and staffing those shows for stage direction, I make it a practice to have someone posted at every exterior and interior entrance, every exit, every green room, dressing area, or hallway corner—everywhere I plan to send, store, or stage talent. If at all possible I keep that person on headset, if only for the one time in the show when either they need to communicate with me or I need to reach out to that position to communicate a change, find a missing member of the cast, light or put out a fire, or revise the show on the fly.

Each of those individuals, long before rehearsals begin, has participated in the production talk-throughs of the script. They know not only their own job, but also the jobs of those that precede, surround, and follow theirs, along with the ramifications of mistakes, missteps, or acts of God. In other words, they know the show. They also serve an often overlooked and quite valuable purpose. There are always those nearly unasked, sometimes whispered (sometimes shouted) questions that need an on-the-spot answer. In other words, this is staffing to keep things smooth and calm and to handle things effectively and seamlessly when things go wrong.

So, take a production that's been talked through and planned amongst the tech and crew. Now add the talent (any person who moves from one part of the stage to another), and here are two possible scenarios:

First, Scenario 1:

Director:

"Alice, darling, walk over to that doorway, would you, and wait 'til we call you for your entrance?"

Alice walks over to the doorway. Touches it, opens it, looks around to see if there are any other doorways, then calls out to the director.

Alice (anxiously; gripping the doorknob):

"This doorway...?"

Director:

"Yep, that one..."

Alice (pointing to the door she is holding with her other hand):

"This one, then?"

Director:

"Yes. Thank you, Alice."

Now Scenario 2:

> Director:
>
> "Alice, darling, walk over to that doorway, would you, and wait 'til we call you for your entrance?"
>
> Alice walks over to the doorway, where she is met by Thomas, standing by the door.
>
> Alice (anxiously, to Thomas):
>
> "This doorway?"
>
> Thomas:
>
> "Yep. Right here."
>
> Alice:
>
> "Thanks!"

Alice is immediately at ease and can ask any other questions of Thomas-the-stage-crew-guy without having to interrupt the director or anyone else. The oblique benefit to this is that she has someone who knows right there with her, while she awaits her cue or direction.

This makes for an exceptionally more relaxed, responsive, and productive team—for both crew and cast. Allow me to clarify that I am not disparaging the talent. Their job is the character, performance, and knowing their stage direction. Offstage, out of their purview, it is only natural that they may be insecure about their perceptions of what has been asked and nervous about simply being where they are supposed to be. Staffing in this way assures confidence.

I am fortunate in that many of my projects are of a level that holds some mystique or glamour, qualities that entice intern-level staffing that are often happy to work for food, the experience, and a place to sleep. While I wouldn't take undue or unfair advantage of kids like that, it is a great opportunity for them to offer themselves to intern and for me to scout future paid crew members. I think everyone wins in these situations, and it starts a lot of young people on the road to their own experience-building pathways.

That being said, I do not believe in asking or making interns work for free. That is, in a practical sense, discriminatory and part of the reason the entertainment industries are predominantly and embarrassingly white and middle/upper class. The cost of supporting these positions is minimal, especially when you see the calmness that results on set and during the show. Especially now, with wireless ClearCom communication systems increasingly affordable, supporting this staffing tool is incalculably valuable. Staffing these types of positions also shows your talent that they are considered valuable. This pays off immensely in relationships, in willingness to collaborate, and in simply taking direction.

Writing this reminds me of when I produced the 40th anniversary of the signing of the Charter of the United Nations at San Francisco's Herbst Theater, where the original charter was signed. There were six of the original signers still living, and we brought them to the ceremony as respected VIP guests to be presented onstage at a major moment during the event.

I don't actually remember why we put them where we did to await their cue; it must have had something to do with the speed at which they could walk and the distance from the stage to the green room. In any event, I had them sequestered and seated backstage, behind a drape in the dark, waiting for my stage managers to come and escort them onto the stage.

As the ceremony began, my right hand guy, John T., came to me and said, "Kile, come here. You've got to take a look at this…" Turning off my headset, I walked back with John, behind the onstage set, and saw The Six, each sitting in the dark, head bowed, hands in laps, awaiting one of the team to come and get them.

"Look how they trust you," he said. "Think who these people are and look how they trust you!"

I have never forgotten that image and what it meant to them and to me. The commitment to keeping my companies at ease remains paramount in my priorities in everything I do.

Thanks, John.

Bonus outtake from Scenario 1:

Alice walks over to the doorway, where she is met by Thomas, standing by the door.

Alice (anxiously, to Thomas):

"This doorway?"

Thomas:

"Yep. Right here."

Alice (taking a good look at Thomas):

"Thanks…um, what's your name? I haven't seen you before…are you new?"

Thomas:

"I'm Thomas. This is my first production with Kile."

Alice:

"Oh, wow; new in town? Perhaps you would like for me to give you a tour sometime? Say, I just had an idea. What are you doing after rehearsal, Thomas?"

...Cut!

Collaboration versus obfuscation

The most valuable information is shared information.

Especially in the context of production teams, it is the responsibility of the producer or production executive to create an environment, a hierarchy, and communications matrix that supports open communication amongst all components of the team. From initial concept development through revision and evolution, it is imperative that all departments participate in the ongoing conversation and process that will lead to the best final result.

Concurrently, the onus is on the representatives of each department, guild, or discipline to respect hierarchy and process, participate in good faith, appreciate the value, talent, experience, and skill of all others at the table, and seek ways in which each can contribute to move the process forward to the best outcome possible.

At first blush this must sound obvious. Yet every so often one can encounter what I call a "hub-and-spoke" producer: one who holds all the cards, all the components, all the information close to the chest and shares bits of information piecemeal—where and when they think it's needed. This means that only one individual has the full big picture. This can slow and even derail the creative and production process(es), effectively keeping those who might well prove to have creative solutions to obstacles in areas other than their own primary purview from contributing.

While the producer or director is the crucial fulcrum for the production and maker of final decisions, they should strive not to hoard.

The simple fact, one that is lost even on the supposedly all-knowing producer, is that not even they have the full picture when they are the only one with all the cards. By not including all others in the process, vast amounts of possibility may never come to light and the final product may suffer in ways never appreciated...as those possibilities were never articulated, examined, or assessed.

I'm sure your mother taught you to share. I'm almost positive she never told you to stop.

Simple solution: regular, inclusive production meetings

At the outset of any project, one of the first things to lock is the schedule of production meetings, even prior to the hiring or appointing of the full team. As individuals or teams are brought on board, that schedule is communicated and individual schedules adjusted to support these regular confabs.

I believe that this full-team practice is critical to the level and quality of success of a show, event, or experience.

My general practice for these meetings is once a week, though a larger scale show or abbreviated production schedule might support twice that. These are calendared and a required commitment of every member of the team for the run of the project. If someone can't make it to a given meeting, they are required to pass along important information or questions to someone conversant in the responsibilities and needs of that department who can make decisions at the meeting.

These meetings are not optional. The entire production or event is reviewed, moment-by-moment, piece-by-piece. Nothing is held back, and any bumps in the road are addressed, any missing pieces discovered and handled. Through this process, far more often as not, missing pieces are discovered, duplications of effort that affect budget are discovered, solutions are offered. The process inevitably produces ad hoc satellite meetings needed to iron out conflicts or forge cooperative teams to address specifics. This is healthy stuff.

This process ensures that every person on the production team becomes aware of where they and their work fit in the production, what is taking place when they are doing their own jobs, what is the Big Picture—what are we creating. This gives a strong and deep sense of ownership and fosters responsibility.

Don't keep people in the dark, intentionally or through ignorance. Include every discipline, even if they are only responsible for a small part of overall design or substance. You just never know.

Share the budget. Allow others to see the budget at these meetings. Not to question where money is spent, but to see through their eyes that they are being supported and to call attention to anything perceived as missing as it is examined. Giving each department or individual the opportunity to review the line items relevant to their responsibilities ultimately protects from coming up short at showtime and having to make last-minute (and more expensive) changes or revisions.

It may also protect the relationship with the client if budgets need to change. Far better to know that way out front than in the final days before curtain.

It is only the inexperienced or unenlightened who complain about money being spent in other areas; that's the producer or director's call. While there's nothing wrong with a little offline lobbying, a clear case made in open forum for money to be well spent will satisfy everyone in the room and alleviate conflict down the road.

Hear the voices of others (beyond those roaming around in your head). Let everyone speak in these meetings or anytime a question arises. Have the patience to let people finish their sentences. Though you might believe you've got a good idea where someone is going in a line of thought or reasoning, you don't actually know until it has been said. Wait for it. Let it be said. You never know what you might hear—and learn—what perspective might change.

Listen.

The Document

Call it what you will: TimeLine, ShowFlow, RunSheet...

This is the single most important document to any production whether one-off, theatrical tour, or permanent installation.

The document begins as a simple list of deadlines:

1. Initiation of processes
2. Building of teams
3. Hiring of principals, professionals, craftspeople
4. Completing designs and scripts
5. Sign-offs and contract signings
6. Scheduling of all key production and all-hands meetings
7. ...all the Big Picture Stuff

But that's just the beginning. As this document evolves, it must gradually encompass every move and position of every component in every moment of the production. Every one. The person who builds this document must be assiduous in going deep—deep into the nuts and bolts of timing and logistics at every level.

This document becomes the very real map of the show.

As the show comes together, each act and scene, each action and speech, is woven into this document. It effectively becomes the working outline for every production meeting, replacing the typical agenda with successive talk-throughs of the production.

This process brings to light each and every duplication of effort, thus saving money and time. It brings parallel needs to the fore, long before load-in or show day, thus saving money and time. It opens the door for creative collaboration amongst talent, craftsmen, technicians, and management...thus saving money, time, and effort, all the while building a strong sense of team and personal investment in the product.

Do not stop there, though. The process and this document remains far from complete without the information on the supporting action that makes each thing happen.

This is where most producers and directors fall short, where most don't go far enough.

Nothing must be assumed. Every action, function, and moment must be timed, responsibility must be assigned, and these, too, woven into the TimeLine such that it becomes clear what is happening—when, where, how, and by whom at Every Single Moment of the Process.

This means that nothing is assumed.

Here's an example:

You have a production assistant who is meeting your talent at the airport. Your TimeLine should reflect:

1. That person's departure from home or office.
2. Arrival at the hotel to pick up the room keys.
3. Arrival at the airport before the flight lands.
4. Estimated delivery to the hotel of said talent.

It continues:

5. Wrangler-initiated wake-up or "I'm on my way to pick you up…" call.

6. Arrival at hotel to pick up talent.

7. Departure from hotel in order to be at the theatre or venue by call time.

8. Delivery to dressing room.

9. Report to stage manager or director that delivery is complete.

So, what is that, nine entries on the TimeLine for one task?

The difference is that most such documents I've seen rarely go further than noting when the talent's flight arrives and when they are expected to show up at the venue.

Not enough.

This thoroughness, carried through to every piece and moment of your show or production, will yield not only a crucial and critically valuable document for the running of the show, but it also gives every single person involved a very clear picture of where their responsibilities lie and how the responsibilities and work of everyone else dovetails with their own.

Be clear on how long each action will take and build your document accordingly. If it takes fifteen seconds to walk from standby position to ready position, then insert that quarter-minute into the TimeLine, accurately. No kidding.

First-time team members who work on my projects,

especially when I am in a new town or country, often laugh when they see listings at 08:45.25, then 08:45.75. The humor is not lost on me; it can be seen as funny. The fact is that these things may well not happen at exactly these times. However, building the TimeLine in this way and to this degree of complexity and specificity will effectively communicate to all involved the critical intricacies of timing and respect for the timing and structure of a show.

Your success will be far greater.

This also gives the show caller or PSM (production stage manager), the producer, and the director the most complete lay of the land as the show unfolds.

Finally, the actual script is dropped into the TimeLine such that, in most of my productions, especially the one-offs, that document becomes the show script. The PSM can drop her cues into the appropriate points and we're good to go. Everyone on the production team has the same document and is in virtual lock-step communication as the show goes up; we're all playing with the same deck.

Something goes wrong?

The executive team has an instant sense of available solutions and alternatives, as each individual is clear as to what resources are available, how far they are from the stage, and how they can reorganize a show on the fly, if that is what is necessary.

There is no substitute for building this document, and it must begin from the first day through final curtain.

The complete TimeLine from our Stanford New York event is included here so you can see exactly what all of this looks like.

TimeLine
for
Think Again! New York

	Tuesday, April 16, 2002			
9:29pm	David Epel arrives UA#890 at JFK			
	Badass Donor Relations Chick calls Grand Hyatt to remind them that we are coming and that EVERY SINGLE NAME on our Master List is to be treated as a "guaranteed late" reservation.		We do NOT want "overflow" at Kile's apartment...	
	Wednesday, April 17, 2002			
5:19pm	Debra Satz arrives EWR aboard UA#906			
5:30	Diane Middlebrook arrives JFK aboard UA#22			
7:51	Laura Carstensen arrives JFK aboard UA#852			
	By day and by night, our Trucks Zoom toward the Northeast en route to NYC For arrival, late tonight...			
	Thursday, April 18, 2002			
All Day	26th Street closed, next to armory			Tabone
6:00am	Load-in Begins Carpet going Down...		ARMORY	Jason Friedman
6:27	William "Bull" Durham arrives JFK aboard UA#4 Just in time for Rush Hour...			
9:00am	Tables and Chairs delivered Donor Relations Sets Up Office at Baruch		26th Street/ Armory Baruch 14-226/227	Abigail Kirsch
1:00 – 3:00pm	"All Hands"/PreCon meeting at Baruch (Catering Maps?)	Convened by KO: In attendance are all Event Principals and "hands-on," onsite managers.	14-226/227 at Baruch	Kile Ozier Donna Garton Donna Robertson Rahela Abbas Margarita Vallin Kristin Baer Sarah Booth Dorothy Law Bob Pringle Michelle Cline John Osthaus BARUCH Principals Chres Coutinho ARMORY Principals Qlydaar/Jackson?

6:00 – 8:30	Centerpiece and Registration Packet Assembly		Armory	Osthaus, Cline and Volunteer Crew
7:00	Parents Dinner with Gerhard Casper and Kathleen Quinn		Knickerbocker Club	
7:51	UA#852 arrives, carrying: Thomas Byers Michelle Mandel James Fox			
8:00	Registration packets move to Baruch			Osthaus
	Friday, April 19, 2002			
12:11	Richard Martin arrives aboard UA#6 at JFK Encounters no traffic – at all – on journey into Manhattan			
All day	Parking Lane closure on 26th Street for Rental Property Trucks Dumpster delivered			Tabone Kirsch
6:00am – 6:00pm	Load-in continues Remaining Rentals Delivered		26th Street	Jason Friedman Kirsch
9:00	**What's Coming UP?** Meeting Port-o-whatever delivered		In Hotel Armory	Stanford Gang of Ten A. Kirsch
1:00	Table lighting focus complete Donor Relations gives approval on placement and lighting Chairs are placed.		Armory	Creative Realities Donna Robertson Kirsch
3:23	UA#28 arrives JFK, carrying David Freyberg and his charming wife, Ann Arvin			
4:00 – 6:00	Media run-through (w/ talent on Saturday afternoon)		Armory	KO Jason Friedman
4:12	David Kennedy arrives LGA aboard USAir#6821			
4:16	Golden Boy Channing Robertson arrives JFK aboard UA#26 Telephones ddr to alert her to his safety and proximity We probably won't see much of them, tonight...			
5:15	Ian Morris arrives JFK aboard American Airlines Flight #202			

Time	Description		Location	Person
5:30	The Mother Lode arrives. UA#22 lands at JFK, carrying: Elizabeth Bernhardt Colt Blacker Valarie Brar Joseph Corn Wanda Corn Damon Jones Chris Maloney Nancy Packer! Everybody's Darling, Bob Ryskamp Ramon Saldivar, the Darling of Many Judith Wasow, (Thomas' Darling?) Thomas Wasow		JFK	Tate
6:30 – 8:30pm	Reception for major-rated CUE donors and prospects: In CT, at the Dennings with G. Casper, J. Ford, D. Lawrence and K. Quinn		Greenwich, CT	Donna Lawrence
8:00	Dinner at Belluna w/ T.L. Boesch Lexington Avenue, between 39/40; near Hotel			Pat Boesch
9:36	UA#862 arrives JFK, carrying: Ernie Young			
	Saturday, April 20, 2002			
12:11	Henry Greely arrives JFK aboard UA#6, and, As Fortune would have it, also encounters absolutely NO traffic, into Manhattan...uncanny.			
6:30	The inimitable John Bravman arrives JFK aboard American Airlines #18			
At this point, it's anyone's guess...	When, at what airport and on what airline Claude Steel will arrive...			
All day	Parking Lane closure for catering trucks			Tabone Kirsch
9:00 – 'til showtime	Donor Relations arrives Final prep for panels and seminars			DR MV, et al

Time	Description		Location	Person
9:01	All **STANFORD** Hands Meeting in **Stanford Office** Accompanied by Breakfast, prepared and organized by John Osthaus...that man's amazing! Not only THAT, but immediately after this meeting and breakfast, Mr. Osthaus will conduct a *personal* tour of the Baruch Facility...not to be missed! (Signs in position, immediately following meeting)		14-226/227	Kile Ozier Donna Garton Donna Robertson Donna Lawrence Rahela Abbas Margarita Vallin Kristin Baer Sarah Booth Dorothy Law Bob Pringle Michelle Cline John Osthaus Michael Tate HHK
11:30	Staff Lunch Signs in Position		14-226/227	John Osthaus
	Minority Alumni Lunch		Grand Hyatt	Julie Lythcott-Haims
12:30	Volunteer Training Begins		Registration Table	Donor Relations
1:00	Faculty meet Pat Boesch/Holly Haley Knapp in Lobby of Hotel To go to Baruch (taxi's, limo's, litters, barge)		Grand Hyatt	Boesch HHK
	Check-in/Registration opens		Foyer: Street Level	Landry-Cline
	Welcome Greeters are in position, wearing their "Kick Me" Buttons – and coat check is ready...		Foyer: Street Level	
1:00 – 5:00	Restrooms transformed from Latrines to Lounges...		Armory	A. Kirsch
1:15	First Guests Arrive too early for early stuff. Fortunately, catering is prepared with light snacks and sodas?		Baruch – Street Level	DR
1:30	Professors begin to arrive for their classes and panels Are shown to their classrooms by staff and volunteers		Baruch	Tate HHK
	Registered Guests move into the damn gym.			DR
1:45	Faculty Introducers arrive at Baruch			HHK Michael Tate

Creative Catalyst

2:25	Greeters move guests to Gym, Except for those excused by notes from Parents...		Baruch – Gym: Level B-2	
2:30	Welcome by **Terry Lindsay** Event Co-Chair Introduction of **Gerhard Casper** Good afternoon and welcome to *Think Again*. Ladies and gentlemen, fellow alumni, parents and friends, my name is Terry Lindsay, class of '78 and today's event chair. It is my pleasure, on behalf of the Stanford Alumni Association and The Campaign for Undergraduate Education, to welcome you to *Think Again* in New York. On behalf of the Stanford family in and around the Big Apple, I would also like to welcome president John Hennessy; John Ford, Vice President for Development; and Howard Wolf, president of the Stanford Alumni Association. (*They will be seated in the front row and will stand to be acknowledged*). Please also welcome all the trustees, faculty, students and staff who have traveled from campus to bring Stanford here to us. Today is a great opportunity for us to not only recall our own Stanford experience, but also to learn what's new in undergraduate education at the university. In fact there is a great deal happening back on The Farm, and we have an amazing program ahead of us. In just a few minutes, we will begin an afternoon of study with some of Stanford's most accomplished faculty. But don't worry – there are no quizzes or blue books! Then, this evening over a seated dinner, we will take a virtual visit back to campus and meet some of today's undergraduates by way of some extraordinary cinematography. You won't want to miss the dinner production. There will be plenty of time to catch up with classmates and meet new Stanford friends as well. But first, to officially convene this Stanford experience, it is my honor to introduce a gentleman who is in many ways responsible for us being here today. From 1992 to 2000, Gerhard Casper served as the ninth president of Stanford University. In that role, one of his many accomplishments was a comprehensive review and renewal of undergraduate education. The outcomes of this review include the remarkably successful program known as Stanford Introductory Studies, about which we will learn and experience much more today. Professor Casper, as he is now known, studies and teaches constitutional law, both at Stanford Law School and in his capacity as the Peter and Helen Bing Professor in Undergraduate Education. He			DTG

also serves as the Convening Co-Chair of The Campaign for Undergraduate Education (called CUE in typical Stanford acronym-speak), which was launched in October 2000 to raise $1 billion exclusively for undergraduate programs and scholarships. CUE and the *Think Again* National Tour are part of Stanford's increased focus on, and indeed renaissance of, undergraduate education – a renaissance for which we have Gerhard Casper to thank.

Please join me in welcoming President Emeritus, Professor and CUE Convening Co-Chair, Gerhard Casper.

(Gerhard gives his Convocation remarks: 6-8 minutes in length. At the conclusion, you will resume the podium and introduce John Bravman)

Thank you Gerhard.

You've just heard about the renaissance in undergraduate education at Stanford, so now let's meet some of today's students that are benefiting from these changes.

To moderate our student panel, is it my honor to introduce a gentleman with a distinguished record of inspiring people to make the most of Stanford. John Bravman first came to The Farm as a freshman in 1975, and has been there almost ever since. He earned his bachelor's, master's, and doctoral degrees at Stanford, all in materials sciences and engineering. He got so much out of Stanford that he was then appointed to the faculty. His research has made him one of the world's leading experts on the properties of thin film materials, such as semiconductors. His work with students has earned him nine awards for teaching, including the appointment he now holds as a Bing Centennial Professor.

Not surprisingly, when then-president Gerhard Casper formed a commission in 1993 to conduct a comprehensive review of the undergraduate experience, John Bravman was a member of that group. John is the dean of the new Freshman-Sophomore College and, most significantly, the Freeman-Thornton Vice Provost for Undergraduate Education. In this last capacity, John oversees all of the new programs, including seminars and increased research opportunities that have revitalized undergraduate education at Stanford.

	Please join me in welcoming Vice-Provost John Bravman.			
2:35	**Bravman** Comments: "Freshman Convocation" Historical context, SIS development, purpose of today's afternoon programs/seminars			
2:45	**Student Panel** – Led by **John Bravman**			
3:29	**John Bravman** sends guests off to school...			DTG
4:00	**Greeters (including Stanford Staff) to all seminar rooms...** **Faculty Presentations**/Introductory Studies Session(s) and Panels. Local host introduces faculty at each seminar... Seminar Schedule/Locations: 5th Floor: 5-150 – Casper/Citizenship 5-165 – Steele 5-160 – Byers 4th Floor: 4-125 – Packer 4-220 – Carstensen 4-225 – Martin 4-180 – Wasow 4-175 – Freyberg 4-185 – Fox 4-213 – Epel 4-160 – Bernhardt 3rd Floor: 3-150 – Morality/Robertson 3-160 – Creativity/Corn 3-165 – Durham 3-125 – Morris		Locations Listed ←	DTG++ DR++
4:45	Wranglers meet VIP Speakers at Turnstile in 24th/Lexington Foyer of Baruch for escorting to Rehearsal			VIPs Wranglers
5:00	Break			DR++
5:00 –	**Rehearsal/Walk-through for All Program Participants**		Armory	Pringle

5:30	**Bob Pringle** wrangles the Speaking VIPs from Baruch to the Armory, where they will... Walk through their entrances and exits; familiarize selves with stage and lectern: A. Charles Ogletree (Pat Boesch) B. Dailey and Gordon Pattee (Bob Pringle) C. Linda Meier (dtg) D. Ward Woods (Donna Lawrence)			Abbas Ozier Donna Robertson Lawrence Boesch Garton
5:30	Repeat of Panels and Seminars Same introduction format			
6:00	All is in readiness in the Reception Area		Second Floor Atrium	DR CATERING
6:25	Afternoon Sessions conclude Staff and Volunteers ready to guide guests to reception Doors open to reception			Cline Robertson Roach, et al
6:30	Reception Officially begins		Atrium	A. Kirsch
	All is in readiness in the Dinner Space			KO/JF++
7:15	Hand Jive Corps meets at bottom of Stairs in Street Level Foyer of Baruch		Baruch to Armory	Cline
7:25	Background Music begins in Dinner space		Armory	KO
	Salads on tables			Donna Robertson/ A. Kirsch
	Flashlight Corps to ARMORY – Marching with Stanford Banners and Foam Hands			MLC
7:28	Images on the screens		Armory	KO
7:30	Doors Open to Dinner		Armory	KO DR++
8:00	House Lights begin to fade As background music begins to build in volume		Armory	KO++
	First Voiceover			KO
	Charles Ogletree to position			Garton
	Intro Ogletree			KO

			Abbas
Ogletree Speaks, Ladies and gentlemen, fellow alumni, students, parents and friends, welcome once more to *Think Again* in New York. I'm Charles Ogletree, class of '74, and I am pleased to see so many members of the Stanford family in the greater New York area here with us tonight. Today's event would not be possible without the enormous dedication, hard work and energy of our volunteers. Led by our wonderful event chair Terry Lindsay, they really made it happen today - from recruitment calls to stuffing packets to introducing faculty to tonight's "foam hand" brigade. We truly could not have done it without them. To see what I mean, please find that little red bag (that you've probably put under your chair) and pull out tonight's program. Now, open it up to the page that says "Thank you, New York" and note all the volunteers that made *Think Again* possible. Will Terry and all these volunteers please stand? Please join me in thanking these wonderful members of the Stanford family. *(They all stand to applause)* The stars of today and this evening are Stanford's faculty and students but not all will be seen. Some will just be heard. Hopefully, you will enjoy the music you are about to hear as well. The Stanford Symphony Orchestra, led by Associate Professor Karla Lemon, performed the music to the film we are about to see. It is an original score, composed for Stanford and recorded at George Lucas's Skywalker Ranch in Marin County. You will hear the symphony's original music again in the final film segment as well. There are 29 undergraduates in the orchestra, *the majority of whom are non-music majors.* In fact, 16 of the 29 are majoring in science or engineering, both which have very demanding course loads. These students are one of many examples you will see and hear about tonight. As bonus for us on the east coast, the orchestra will perform at Carnegie Hall on June 18 as a kick-off for the European tour. I hope you will plan to hear and support our students "live and in person" at that time. As we begin tonight's program, please direct your attention to the two screens on either side of me. Throughout the evening and when the lights go down, the film segments will take place on both screens at the same time and you won't want to miss any of it. Now, please join me as we go back to The Farm. Thank you. then is escorted back to his table by the chocolate-haired Rahela...			

8:15	**House** goes dark as score begins (v/o) **Opening Segment** Runs (5 minutes)			KO
	Hennessy to offstage position			Robertson
8:20	**Opening Segment** concludes/**House lights** up to "ambience" as			KO
	Hennessy steps onto stage from Stage Right welcomes the audience to Stanford, and gives comments			Abbas/ Robertson
	No service at tables during Hennessy			A. Kirsch
8:30	**Hennessy** completes remarks			
	Service Resumes with collection of Salads			Kirsch
8:35	**House lights** down as **Voiceover obliquely introduces** **Undergraduate Insights** (yet somehow captures the attention of all guests...) And segment commences (10 minutes)			KO
	No Service during film			A. Kirsch
8:43	**Dailey and Gordon Pattee** escorted to standby position, stage right			Donna Robertson
8:45	**House Lights** back to "ambience" as **Undergraduate Insights** concludes,			KO
	Service Resumes as Pattees begin to speak			A. Kirsch
	Pattees approach Lectern: speak Good Evening. I am Dailey Pattee, class of '71, (or I am Gordon Pattee, class of '70; or we are...your call from now on) and also parent of Mary Dailey, class			Abbas

	of '03 and Ashleigh, class of '06. I don't know about you, but I am in awe of those undergrads. They are but a small sample of today's Stanford students. As you might imagine, there are many students from the greater New York area represented in the films tonight:		
	Leah Brunski from Niskayuna, Sarah Clowes from Rochester, Peter Koob from Riverside, Connecticut; Tim Meyer from Guilford, Connecticut; Daniel Nidzgorski from Basking Ridge, New Jersey; and Iris Zimmerman from Rush, New York.		
	We are very fortunate to have many of their parents with us tonight. As I read your names, would you please stand? Please welcome Betsy and John Brunski, Pam and Chuck Koob, and Connie and Felix Nidzgorski, (They all stand to applause.)		
	Speaking of Stanford parents, I would like to welcome two, particularly special couples that play such an important role on the Parents' Advisory Board. Please join me in thanking Karen and Ed Hsu from New York and Tina and Paul Schmid from Boston, as well as all the New York area members of the board for their service to Stanford. Would you all please stand? Thank you. (They all stand to applause.)		
	Finally, please also welcome Leslie and George Hume from San Francisco, alumni and parents of Parker, class of 2000. Leslie is a current trustee and George a former trustee; and, importantly for us, they are serving as campaign vice-chairs for parents. Please welcome the Humes. (They stand to applause)		
	Now please enjoy your dinner and your dinner companions. Toward the end of the main course you're in for a real treat. You will meet some more of today's students as we will be joined on the screens by some of Stanford's finest student, a cappella groups. One of the groups, The Mendicants, will serenade us in a most unusual way - so pay attention to the lights and the screens on the stage.		
	Thank you.		
	Hosts descend stage via Stage Left Stair, met by **Rahela Abbas**		
8:46.5	**Main Course** is served WHILE **Pattees** are speaking Many introductions...		DR CATERING
8:46.5 – 9:30	**Dinner** happens Guests chat and chew		DR++ KO/JF

9:17	**Stanford Harmonics virtual performance**		
9:20	**Soloist** is ready – at table #		KO
9:23	**Mendicants** Sing "Brown-Eyed Girl" Live soloist		KO/JF
9:27	Wild applause from audience As applause crests...		
9:28.5327	**House lights** fade to black Ryskamp "informal" intro of Casper "inspiration" and Academic Segment Casper voiceover		KO
9:29	**Academic Segment** commences		KO
9:29.5 – 9:39	During **Academic Segment**, **Catering** swiftly creeps about the room, replenishing wine and water, silently **collecting the dinner plates**; stacking nothing, making no noise at all...no one even notices them...Kirsch totally rocks.		Donna Robertson CATERING
9:39	With one minute to go, **Linda Meier** is escorted to her standby position, stage right.		DTG
9:40	**Academic Segment** concludes Voiceover: "Ladies and Gentlemen, Linda Meier" Stage up as **Linda Meier** Steps into Spotlight		KO KO DTG/Abbas
9:40.25	**Linda Meier steps to lectern** As we have just seen as well as experienced this afternoon, Stanford is blessed with an incredible faculty; and twenty-four of the university's finest professors have joined us in New York. While they all stand as a group, please join me in thanking these dedicated and gifted members of the Stanford family. (They stand to applause.) And would our four undergraduates also please stand? Valarie Brar, Damon Jones, Chris Maloney, and Bob Ryskamp. (They stand to applause)		DTG/Abbas DTG/Abbas

Creative Catalyst

	Now if you think the evening is complete, *Think Again!* We have a brief film segment you won't want to miss, followed by a delicious dessert. So please remain seated and enjoy the rest of the evening		
9:44	**Brief Remarks from Linda Meier** conclude, to much applause **Meier** descends via stairway, Stage Left (met by Rahela Abbas), as		Abbas
9:44.25	**House Lights** down... and **Closing Segment** commences **NO SERVICE** during film		KO KO A. Kirsch
9:50	**Ward Woods** to standby position, Stage Right		Robertson
9:52	**Closing Segment** completes Pin Drops All hear it...Well, they DO!		KO Awestruck Guests
9:52.25	**Voiceover,** "Ladies and Gentlemen, Mr. Ward Woods		KO
9:52.5	**Ward Woods** appears **Onstage to make** Closing Remarks – (CATERING waits on periphery with a Wonderfully Decadent Dessert...) Wow! Aren't we all fortunate to be part of such an incredible place? As a member of the class of '64 and a university trustee, I also believe that Stanford is the best university in the world. Thank you for coming. Thank you for caring about our *alma mater*. We hope today's event has renewed your Stanford spirit and that your relationship with the university is lifelong, rewarding and mutually supportive. As Linda Meier mentioned earlier, please enjoy this wonderful dessert, your dinner companions, and your memories of The Farm. However, when you leave, please remember to take home your chocolate lollipops and red Stanford bags. Thank you.		Robertson
9:54	**Background Music** throughout Room		KO JF++

9:54++	**Audience** uses room as **Reception Area** for post-event dessert and coffee, networking and Sharing of astonishment at having the privilege of being of Stanford and being here, tonight...		DR++
10:30 or, whenever they're ready...	Faculty returns to Grand Hyatt		
11:00	Doors close to ARMORY, as Donor Relations sweep ARMORY for favors left-behind, and ... Breakdown and staging for Load-out begins Carpet Vacuumed Way cleared for Health Fair on Sunday		KO Donna Robertson JF++ A. Kirsch
	Sunday, April 21, 2002		
All Day	All Depart		ALL
	Monday, April 22, 2002		
	26th Street closed for Load-out		Tabone CR
	Thursday, April 25, 2002		
9:00am PDT Noon EDT	De-Briefing at Stanford		ALL

Contribute to the process and the process will support you

This goes for everyone on the team, from top to bottom and side to side. Hierarchy is not bureaucracy, it is structure: a framework that should be designed so that every component of the team can depend on the others. Without hierarchy and fulcrum, there is no organization. Things fall through the cracks, unnecessary money is spent, departments find themselves unsupported, people, and clients, get cranky.

Trust department heads to do their jobs and alert you to problems in plenty of time. If you are a department head, be clear about the support you need and that which you offer. Production meetings are the perfect forum to ask for support where it's needed, and to offer the same.

Then, if hierarchy becomes bureaucracy, burn it down and begin again.

Ultimately, creative, production, and budgetary decisions are most effectively made by a single individual, whether that be the producer, director, or other.

This fact of hierarchy must remain sacrosanct, being held as such by every member of the team. I have found, in my own experience, that the more fully my teams have participated in the creation of a project, the more willing they are to live with and actively, authentically support the decisions made by the one in charge when all is said and done.

Creative Catalyst

Working with talent

Have a plan and be prepared

When directing the candlelight vigil for the National AIDS Memorial Quilt at the Lincoln Memorial in 1992, the iconic Joel Grey offered me an experience that taught me much in mere moments.

The first time I'd met him was the day before the event, when he arrived for sound check. I was just some young guy from L.A. while he was pretty much my first A-level celebrity performer. I introduced myself. He said, "Are you the director?" "Yes, I am." "What would you like me to do?"

Of course, the piece he was to perform had already been agreed. So, respectfully and clearly, I said, "Well, Mr. Grey, here's how I had envisioned this piece, this moment, unfolding…" and proceeded to walk him through where I wanted him to stand, to move, to time the verses, and explained the giant, absolutely silent skyrocket that was to punctuate the end of his performance and close the show.

"What do you think, Mr. Grey?"

I was ready for him. And I was ready to compromise, capitulate, to submit, and be told how he would do it. That is not what happened.

What he said was, "Great. Then, that's what I'll do!" One rehearsal and we were done.

What I learned from that encounter was: a true professional looks to the director to understand the vision, and trusts that the director knows the Big Picture and how each performance plays into that.

So. Be confident. Don't act confident; be confident. Know your show, know why you have made the decisions you have made, placed components where you've placed them, written entrances in the manner and position(s) in which you have done so. It is only the insecure artist who will make trouble and insist on things that may not work inside your vision. Beware of making any artists insecure through communicating doubt, through not knowing an answer, or for simply being obsequious.

Frankly, a director who is starstruck should be in some other business, not dealing with talent. A professional can sniff out an amateur a mile away—then you'll see who calls your shots! Be confident, be patient, ask for advice, and listen to your talent if they are compelled to offer suggestions. Talent may well know how they might look their best, but you are in charge of the show. A pro will collaborate. You may have to take a hard line on someone whose ego might supercede their entertainment value. Take that line or risk exposing your show to sacrifice.

Keep the speeches short

You know what I mean. Nobody likes a filibuster, and a monologue is only good in theatre. When building a program for an event, one of the most egregious sins is that of losing control of the guest speakers. This results in the dissipation of audience attention, which usually heralds the loss of interest on the part of the suffering audience.

Creative Catalyst

There is consequence to making an audience suffer.

"Three minutes" sounds short. Three minutes is not short. A great and contextually enlightening exercise when working with speakers (or for oneself) is to suggest holding one's breath for one full minute just to see how long that feels.

There's your rule of thumb. Further, telling a speaker "three to five minutes" generally results in twice that... or more. Telling a speaker "one minute...okay, 90 seconds," and then negotiating an additional 30 seconds will impress on the speaker that you mean what you say and result in a better speech that is embraced far more by the audience. Winnowing one's speech to less than three minutes, more often than not, results in the most powerful, clear, compelling, and resonant delivery of message. A lot can be said in this amount of time.

In 2011 I worked on a signature event with an organization, focused on messaging and evolving the "program" part of the evening into a tight and powerful seventeen minutes. This seventeen minutes included ALL the speaking parts (welcome, acknowledgments, thanks, introduction of honoree, honoree) as well as the entertainment component, which by itself was four minutes long.

Four minutes. This can be done.

The speakers had been unambiguously apprised of the importance of keeping the program brief and pithy and were well aware of their respective constraints. Underscoring the seriousness of the parameters, each speaker or performer could see me in clear view, standing adjacent to the stage and prepared to step onto the stage, grab the microphone and thank them mid-overrun. While this resulted in good-natured ribbing from the lectern, the parameters were respected.

This is your job as executive in charge of any such production—any production—to ensure the message is delivered and the audience is happy. No single component or participant in a theatrical production, ceremony, celebration, or simple program trumps the importance of the audience experience. None.

The 2011 event was a huge success; the word on the street for the ensuing year was "you should have been there." As a result, tickets exceeded sell-out the following year.

In 2012, however, that same organization chose to relinquish all parameters and advisories to the speakers, resulting in over 45 minutes of speeches in a three-hour stand-up event. This was in addition to the entertainment portion of the experience. Nearly one-third of the evening was given over to the presenters and honorees, with the rationale given that the organization's leadership didn't want to offend those special guests in the room that evening.

This proved to be a very costly capitulation. Virtually all the reviews of that evening cited the oppressive length of the speeches, lamely concluding, "...otherwise, it was fine."

"You should have been there!" versus, "...otherwise, it was fine."

Creative Catalyst

When you've done it right...

A few years ago I heard from a friend and former colleague whom I'd enticed into this business after having worked with and observed his meticulousness at Apple. Keith might be called a protégé, having worked with me for the duration of two projects. He's a fast learner, and in no time was on his own making new history in Dubai. In short order he became Director of Entertainment at Yas Waterworld, one of the two highest-ranked water parks in the world. He's a natural.

Anyway, for the few months prior to our conversation he'd been working on the debut of a brand-new character, diver, and acrobat-driven water show. It had premiered the day before, and I was excited to learn how it went.

"So? How'd it go?"

"Well," he said. "The show opened yesterday, and guess what I did?"

"I don't know; tell me! Took notes? What?"

He looked me right in the eye as a big smile grew on his face and he said, "Nothing!"

I was honored, flattered, and kind of proud to witness it.

12

Time

So, let's talk for a moment about time. It truly is of the essence, in every respect.

When putting an experience together, be it theatrical, spectacle, industrial, or guerrilla, it's important to remember that every moment communicates something. The key is to be sure that each and every moment that occurs between curtain up and end of show communicates what you want it to.

Every. Moment.

When crafting an experience, it is critical to be aware not only of the overall timing of each scene or component, but also the silences, the quiet, the transitions in between action as well as each scene and act. As most creatives are aware, the space between successive speeches in a script can compellingly communicate mood, dynamic, and tone, giving a sense of subtext and backstory, nuance.

Nuance. Makes or breaks an experience.

My mantra in this context is "No Dead Air." Every moment is planned and foreseen.

Never make an audience wait; rather, make them anticipate. The difference is key—to wait is to be distracted, to leave the story arc or narrative, to exit the experience and wonder what and when. To anticipate, though, is about reaching for what's next, being engaged, mentally percolating possibility and reaching out to grasp The Next Thing...

Use any silence to communicate something—tension, time passing, surprise. Let nothing "just take as long as it takes." Instead, write the pauses and transitions into your show or experience. Pay close attention to the pacing, then assiduously keep the integrity of that pace or rhythm. This sometimes means covering something as basic as a scene change with a voice-over, some activity in another part of the space, or even something as simple and basic as a lighting or sound effect. It's gotta make sense, and it has to fit.

As creators we need to remain wary of what we might be accepting. Of course the set and scene needs to change; it may not, though, have to stop the action or impede the storytelling in order to do so.

Controlling time

Another facet of time and timing is restraint.

Holding back.

A major part of what I do is create and direct ceremonies: sports, awards, acknowledgments, and recognition. In this context, an historical parallel or ancestor might be the old-fashioned variety show, but enhanced and augmented with a theme, through-line and purpose beyond simply entertaining. The parallel that is reflected in these ceremonies is the "parade" of what is often a succession of talented individuals or small groups paying tribute to a person or institution through their talent.

Don't let the talent ru(i)n the show.

These people will always want to do more than might be envisioned, to showcase themselves such that it may detract from the power of the overall experience. For instance, the divas will want to do at least two numbers, the monologuists always need five to seven minutes, and the dancers must showcase their every signature move. As much as we may love each bit someone pitches for inclusion, we do not put them all onstage.

Just a note on acknowledging the negative generalizations in the preceding paragraph: not all talent are blind to the bigger picture, and of course talent should push hard to give the best show that they can. It comes from the heart (and self-preservation) and should be appreciated by the director and producer as such. That being said, as the shepherd of the vision, responsible for audience response, it is up to leadership to maintain boundaries and see to it that the sum IS greater than the parts. Boundaries. Big Picture. Holding the line.

The talent often sees only their individual contribution, giving lip service to the importance of timing in the overall production. But in their heart of hearts they pretty much consider themselves the centerpiece.

This is where the person in charge of creation—the producer, the director, the creative director—must be brutally judicious. I learned early on that keeping segments almost uncomfortably short was more often than not a good barometer for any audience's reception, that it was the right move and created the best overall effect. For once a piece or segment has gone on too long, it is virtually impossible to resurrect the energy that may have been lost. Select one song, keep the dance number short, minimize the monologues and speeches. So much can be communicated in a very short time and, in a marginal concession to the world in which we live, we need to create experiences that reach out and repeatedly capture and recapture attention.

Don't pack your show. Two short, powerful speeches or moments can be a one-two punch: communicative and effective. Add just one more of these and all three can immediately become too long, losing the energy and losing your audience. Not everyone who "needs" to speak needs to speak. Be strong. Hold the line on length, on transitions, on quietness; give people enough to engage them, not sate them.

As director or producer, our job is the integrity of the show or program, seeing that the message is delivered sans distraction or obstruction and as evocatively or compellingly as possible. The experience of the audience is the single most important criterion—more important than the happiness of the speaker, the performer, the sponsors, and the caterer.

It's quite a tightrope. If anybody's not happy, on either side of the stage, then you are risking the quality of experience you most want for your audience. What it takes is commitment to the best delivery of the experience on the part of the creators, along with a stage manager who appreciates that they are responsible for seeing to it that plans are appreciated, understood, accepted, and kept.

Getting it done

More often than not a microphone can be like a drug to the talent. Once a performer gets one in their hands, it can be as though the mic and the performer are one. That mic can become remarkably difficult to wrest out of a grip of a diva. For politicians and social leaders this dynamic seems almost genetic and built-in.

So...how?

Here are a pair of anecdotes from which I learned in a practical way how important adherence to program timing—and the value of brief, tight, pithy programs—adds value and keeps the integrity of an experience.

Way back in the pre-web dark ages I was producing an event for a high-end group of political donors in Northern California. The only speech that stood between the guests and their dinner was that of a State Representative from the area, known behind-the-scenes as a tad long-winded. His speech was slated for five minutes. In a pre-show conversation I raised that time constraint and he nodded. I was young and relatively inexperienced; I thought we had an agreement and didn't worry about it.

Later, as he passed the ten-minute mark with no signs of slowing down, I took things into my own hands. On headset, I said to my stage managers who were holding the closed doors to dinner, "Hmm....I think I might be having trouble with the sound, here...something's funky...be prepared to respond to me, just in case..."

I then turned off his microphone.

He began smacking the mic and gesticulating to me that he was having sound trouble. I nodded, held up my hand in the "wait" signal and looked to be fiddling with the board as I said into my ClearCom, "Open the doors."

Creative Catalyst

As the doors opened I looked back across the room to him and held up my hands in a, "Wow, I have no idea why you don't have sound" gesture as the audience rapidly flooded into the dining room. That anteroom was cleared within about two minutes. Happy audience, mood and energy preserved.

The client came over to me to commiserate. "Damn, too bad about the sound...but I don't know if he'd ever have stopped speaking, otherwise..."

It's always easier to apologize than to ask permission.

Getting down to it

Here's how to build a program that is pithy, compelling, and entertaining—and how to make sure that it remains that way.

STEP ONE: Take a deep breath. Hold it for one full minute.

STEP TWO: Okay, nice try. Try it again. Deep breath. Keep it in! ONE FULL MINUTE!

STEP THREE: Yeah, right? Not so easy, is it? One minute is a loooong time.

So, there's your reference, your building block. As you build or write a show, remember how long a single minute is. So, as you tell your performers or speakers that they have three minutes, two minutes, even as seemingly brief as a one-minute introduction, you are not limiting them. Rather, you are offering them an opportunity to deliver something powerful, direct, and memorable. Your audiences will appreciate this restraint and discipline without actually knowing of it.

Step four: Delivery is key. Inform your performers and speakers how much time they have; do not ask them. Set their expectations and share the importance of respecting the overall experience. There is a marked difference between:

> **Could you please try to keep your comments to about three... three and a half minutes? You know, we want to keep the program tight and if you could keep yours short, that'd be great. If you go to four, no big deal, just keep it under five, okay...?**

and

> **We are very tight for time on this program and you are the main part of it. It is important that we keep your segment to three minutes. Will you do that? Three minutes. I'll give you a signal at 2:30.**

The moment you offer leeway is the moment that your speaker or performer thinks they're Bill Clinton or Barbra Streisand. There is nothing wrong with a one-minute intro or a three-minute speech. This works in everyday life. For instance:

- Most pop songs are under three minutes
- Operatic arias
- The Pledge of Allegiance
- Late-night monologues
- Marriage proposals
- Wedding vows
- Even multi-million dollar television commercials are thirty seconds

Creative Catalyst

Singers will always want to perform one more song than the one you've requested, comics another joke or character, speakers another minute or ten...Do not accept this.

Make it fun and make it *happen*

So after all that, you want to know how easy it actually is to do this? Very easy.

From the outset, one must be confident, definite, and respectful of the parameters of time to which you are committed. Communicate fully and completely and with a smile. Offer to help with speechwriting if that is in your skill set. Most professionals will respect you and your position and follow accordingly.

Some, of course, will find themselves incapable of keeping within a given time constraint. This, too, is easily addressed. My basic approach, which I make clear in our first meeting, is:

- There will be a light or some signal from the back of the house at thirty seconds to wrap.
- At fifteen seconds to wrap, I (or my trusty stage manager) will appear at the edge of the stage, offstage, or just below the stage in very plain sight of the speaker.
- At five seconds, I will be clearly approaching the lectern, ready to take the mic, thank the speaker, and introduce the next act or component of the show.

I have rarely had to actually step in and take the mic, but have always been clearly and obviously ready to do so. More often than not, it becomes a joke that is shared with the audience. "I see my time is about up…" or, "Uh-oh, here comes Kile with the hook…" And all continues swimmingly.

You simply must be confident and not intimidated by or afraid of your talent or speakers. They are depending on you to deliver an experience as designed and envisioned. An ego or two may occasionally be ruffled, though with the mitigating upside that you'll be appreciated by your audience and ultimately thanked by your audience.

You'll also probably develop a reputation for running tight shows. That's worth money.

Exceptions? Certainly.

You have a singer who brings down the house? Give them an encore. Maybe bring her back at the end of the program in response to an unplanned, audience-wide wish for more. This exceeds expectation in a way that still respects the integrity of the show or story arc you have created, while offering the proverbial "more" in an unexpected way.

All of this should be flexible, given the specifics and particulars. But you keep on top of it. The moments in shows that to this day continue to give me chagrin and regret are when I caved to an additional song, a third recital, one more speech that resulted in dragging down the experience of the entire program.

Do not cave (though, always consider). Your job is the result.

"Always leave 'em wanting more…" is not fiction. Build that into your experience. Inspire them to return.

Creative Catalyst

13

Listening

S ome years ago at the end of my first gig in Dubai, one of the well-seasoned production coordinators pulled me aside in front of her team at the wrap lunch prior to my departure and said to me, "You know, we get a lot of consultants around here"—meaning, I believe, older white guys with grey hair—"but you are different. You know what sets you apart?

"You listen…"

I appreciated that acknowledgment at the time, though in my heart of hearts I really did not think that listening could be so unusual. After all, the value of listening before opening one's mouth is no mystery…or so I surmised.

I make it a habit to strive to be sure that everyone in a given meeting has spoken before I weigh in, if for no other reason than to know the lay of the land, to get a sense of everyone's perspective, to gain a sense of who may feel invested with a strong opinion and may not feel heard. It's a great way to suss out the interpersonal dynamic and glean the "energy history" of a project or team.

If I'm the guy running the meeting, it's easy to make sure we hear from everyone. If I'm asked a question that relates to the purview of someone else, I first turn to that person for history and point of view. Everyone comes out of such a meeting better informed and a stronger team, even if they don't realize it at the time.

This is just good. Empowering (to the team), enlightening (to the leaders) management practice.

After first contact I make it a point to follow up, especially with lower levels of management and staff, or

Creative Catalyst

with those with hands-on responsibility. I want their opinions on the meeting and what may have been missed or overlooked. These conversations almost always pay off in knowledge and relationships for the run of the project...and beyond.

People need to be heard.

Knowing one has been heard immediately relaxes the "inbound portals" of the psyche, and the individual begins to hear better and more effectively, contribute more productively, and truly feel part of a team.

As leader or member of the team, one never knows what one is likely to learn by simply hearing.

On another occasion I was saying my goodbyes to some of the professionals in the company with which I had been consulting. I heard it, again.

> You know, for an American...
>
> I gotta say one thing about you...
>
> I sure wish more consultants were like you...
>
> So many of these guys come in and think they know everything and just start throwing their opinions around as though they are some sort of unquestionable treasure...

And you know what, they're right. Over the past few years, as I've watched consultants parachute into foreign situations with the idea that they are going to "straighten things out," I have come to appreciate why consultants so often have a bad name and are received with suspicion by the rank and file.

It's the white knight syndrome.

The consultants in question are known for sweeping in on brooms with fairy dust to launch right into solution mode. Allow me to paraphrase:

Well, here's what's wrong...

That's not the way to do it...

Do it THIS way...

Over at D*sney, where I used to hang out with J*e as we built X Famous Project...

By the way, dropping names of iconic projects, companies, and people tends to alienate others on your team. Discretion will greatly serve you when your impressive relationships are discovered obliquely, if discovered at all, and earn even more respect for having been discreet.

Rarely have I witnessed a star consultant initiate conversation with questions about how the team got to this point, what the history of the project might be, what the original vision was, what was behind the decision to do something. All too often the hot-shot expert seems intent on making a mark on the project at the soonest possible moment.

Do not make this mistake. Plan to stand on your talent, experience, and skill; what you bring to the table will be what impresses others and inspires confidence—never who you know. Even the Lone Ranger would ask a lady if she needed help before he'd just ride in and grab her. Well, most of the time...but you get my point.

I also see a rather condescending assumption that, "The natives just don't get it..." because they are not smart...rather than the more likely possibility that something cultural might be in the way. People think in different ways in different parts of the world; not everything can be readily translated into Western ways of thinking or even understood by Western thinkers. Some things simply must be embraced and worked with rather than dismissed as "wrong."

I see a lot of condescension and dismissal among consultants, and I don't know if they realize just how much of that is so clearly seen and experienced by the clients. It ain't all that discreet, actually. Our value comes in what we have learned and what we know and how we impart that information in a way that can be used. Our respect must be authentic.

I used the euphemism of "parachuting" into a situation. A real parachutist actually spends no small amount of time studying the lay of the land before leaping out of the plane. She has a firm grasp of where solid ground is, where the roads are, which bridges are intact or burned, and as much an appreciation of the regional language as might be possible before jumping in to solve a problem.

I don't see the army of Western consultants doing that. (I do know some who do, and do it well; these are heroes.) I've simply been surprised at the otherwise-intelligent people who don't study the host culture and its ways of communicating and doing business as something to embrace and learn rather than something to "fix." Most often it can't be "fixed." Nor should it be.

Here's the thing. It's easy to impress the money guys—the CEOs, the CFOs, the C-suite executives—with pedigree from the highest levels of experience from the Western leaders in theme parks. But to really affect the flow of a project, to have a positive effect on the team, process, and result, one must know one's team and be respected by that group.

The Western way isn't the only way. Nor is the Disney or Universal way the only way. There are myriad "Western" ways, many of which have roots in the East. Open up!

As with salt, I suppose.

Salt is, like, the best thing to ever happen to food (right?!). But too much salt, or salt by itself, will yield something inedible, unworkable. Perhaps our Western approach is the salt we bring to themed entertainment. And, just as there is no one salt, there is no single Western way to do things. Each of us brings different backgrounds, skills, and talents to the table and create differently applicable solutions for the projects we address. Judiciously and effectively applied, the Western point of view can yield the best possible result or contribute to it, but one cannot dismiss the host culture.

What is productive is listening. Listening with eyes and ears. Listening with respect. Watching the body language of the team members at every level. Openness toward being shown how best one can help a project happen, a vision become realized.

I recently watched a strong business relationship crumble, solely from not listening and hearing. The principal of the consulting firm suddenly quit, after nearly twenty years with that firm and after having been the primary communications conduit between them and the client company since the inception of the business relationship. This shot the relationship off balance and caused much alarm within the client company, now concerned that he was going to their competition.

He assured them he was not going to the competition. And then he went to the competition. It caused further frustration and unrest in the client company.

Unfortunately, the client's deep consternation was met with stonewalling on the part of the consulting firm. The importance of building and maintaining (or rebuilding triage) of personal business relationships didn't seem to have the same level of importance for the two parties.

Exploration of assumption

Remember, you are being invited to come to this other place, into this other house, to join this other team because you have been successful on similar things in the past. The requirement is not that you are to show up with the answers; the theory is that you will know how to find the way in what is always a unique situation and confluence of circumstance and fact.

In fact, thinking one is showing up with the answers is just being arrogant and letting down the client.

So before offering any solutions:

- Ask questions.
- Be respectful.

- Ask advice.
- Build the team.
- Ask more questions.
- Curb the ego. You are there because you are good. No need to remind anyone.
- No project is cookie-cutter, not from barn to barn, stage to stage, park to park, and certainly not from country to country.
- Strive to balance teaching with learning for you and the team and discover how happy and productive your team becomes.

You'll likely be pleased with the result.

Focused listening informs the response.

The key thing to keep in mind about listening is that it virtually always informs.

We all know what we "know." If we can remember that what we may not know might change what we "know," I believe it becomes far easier to set aside one's own point of view with each encounter until one has fully heard the other side of the conversation, be that

- One's partner
- One's collaborator
- One's manager or employee
- One's teammate
- Everyone in the room

Creative Catalyst

This means, in real terms, maintaining the discipline of not making assertions and not operating under assumption until one has truly heard the other side. Not scripting one's response or next statement until after that other side has shared their point of view.

For it is that moment between hearing and speaking in which will be born the most germane, the most authentic, the most productive question or response. Give it that moment. Allow the response to be born. More often than not I have found that what I thought I would share or ask has changed and become more productive and positive after having actually heard.

The best actors, despite the fact that the scene is scripted, memorized, and rehearsed, listen each night to their colleagues on the boards. They listen as though their character is hearing this for the first time and thus respond authentically.

It is remarkable how well this works in real life.

14

Professionalism

came across this bit of ridiculousness in a LinkedIn post:

Confidence: fake it 'til you make it! Nobody wants an insecure leader or employee. If you don't know what you are doing, act like you know what you're doing until you know what you are doing. Preparation is key because when you prepare, you feel genuinely confident and others trust that you know what you are doing because…well, you do. Attitude is everything, and the mind achieves what the mind believes.

Bunk.

This is what got Wall Street into trouble; this is a gung-ho "sales team of the '70s" attitude that undermines credibility and depletes integrity from any environment. A leader who "fakes" knowledge and experience—in any industry and specifically in production, show, and entertainment—is not a leader at all. Such a person is phony, and it ultimately shows in the quality of the product and be reflected in the attitude of their team.

The second sentence is true, actually—nobody wants an insecure leader. Ironically in this case, an exceptionally pithy example of insecurity is a manager or ostensible leader who is "faking it."

As a leader, one is much better off being secure in what one does not know, knowing where to find things and learning how to apply what they discover. Learning alongside your team engenders an authentic, profound respect from them. A leader who can learn teaches humility and learning ability. A leader who fakes it

Creative Catalyst

teaches his team to lie. (...and probably laugh behind his back at his delusion that anyone is being fooled...)

In my business, there are producers who are known for acting as though they know everything about production. These guys get in the face of lighting designers, production coordinators, choreographers, composers, riggers, and stagecraft professionals and attempt to second-guess the work and process of those who've spent years focused on the areas of theatre to which they are committed...committed to being the best at what they do.

Those producers are producers who give real producers a bad name.

A real producer knows to stand back, to inspire their experts and let them do their best work, knowing when good work is being done and supporting the team in doing it. A leader inspires, embraces learning, learns from the people on her team, and keeps the team moving in the right direction, eyes focused on the ultimate vision of the show.

Nobody knows everything about production. Everyone brings experience, knowledge, and passion to their jobs. A leader learns of that experience and seeks to benefit from it; a leader appreciates the knowledge his team members bring to the table and embraces the passion with which that knowledge is applied.

This doesn't mean not to give your people instructions—not at all. Clear communication of vision, goals, and objectives is key to success. Further, asking professionals how they are accomplishing the work is often appreciated...when the question is based in seeking knowledge (rather than seeking some sort of "advantage"). Collaboration alleviates obfuscation, nurtures and incites creativity, and strengthens relationships.

More often than not everyone on the team appreciates being asked about what they do, sharing their own knowledge and experience. Asking them is acknowledging their expertise. It shows appreciation for the work and focus those team members put into being the best at what they do.

Learn from your team. The decisions you make, your artistic, logistical, and even dramaturgical choices will be the better for it.

So, rather than "fake it 'til you make it..." How about...

Learn it and you'll earn it.

Professional business conduct

There is an ever-changing, evolving set of procedures and responsibilities that support productive and clear communication between professionals as we work together both in real time and in cyberspace. An increasing number of individuals have grown up with the web as part of their daily world. They just take it for granted, and yet the rules that apply to our communication with one another will continue to evolve.

With this in mind, knowing it will change yet again, I offer some guidelines for successful relationship-building and maintenance in a wired and wireless world.

The first thing to remember is that not everyone in our industries is the same age, nor is everyone of any age necessarily at the same level of technological ability at any given time. Increasingly, middle-aged and older individuals are embracing the web and relinquishing old habits of communicating. Younger folks will see more potential success and welcome remembering that what they and their peers are so used to doing might seem rude or even ignorant to others—people with whom they just might want to forge relationships or even get a job from someday.

Take nothing for granted. Often a few extra seconds of thought when communicating will reap bountiful rewards. Some of the smartest, most accomplished people in these industries are still just a tad intimidated by the web, simply out of unfamiliarity with it. Even the most respected hero may shy away from unfamiliar territory, having little or no experience with these tools, platforms, and formats used for communication and collaboration.

Everyone will get there in the long run. But, until everyone who is now in their 20s reaches 40 and 50, there will still be those with whom they want to work and learn from, who require sensitivity to their separate learning curves. And by the way, when those age milestones are reached, things will have evolved yet again—the cycle continues as the next set of youngsters show up at the front door.

Inherent in this are some old rules of communication that, while evolving, will be helpful to keep in mind. In no particular order:

Personalize your communication

When seeking to connect on an online platform, using the default "I'd like to join your network" message is often seen as rude, dismissive, or just plain lazy.

Take a moment to send a message to the individual, saying you are going to send them a friend or link request and would appreciate their consideration. Less than a minute for a sentence or two will help you shine over the pack and likely be remembered at a crucial time in the future that may involve opportunity.

I used to just ignore people on FaceBook and LinkedIn who sent the request without taking time to write a personal note. I have now capitulated, finding it easier to just accept current culture, though not without unease. Given that LinkedIn is a professional networking site, before I give someone access to my network I would prefer to know where they work and how they know me. Each time I receive a prefab LinkedIn request that says, "Because I trust you…," I have to chuckle. This person doesn't know me—how can they trust me?

You know who stands out? The ones who send me a note. One sentence: "I saw you speak at…" "I read your post on…" Simple, easy, eminently memorable.

Find ways to personalize; it will serve you.

Maintain contact

As you network, and as you benefit from that network, stay in touch with your contacts and especially with your mentors. If you get advice from someone:

Do not fail to thank them in writing.

Creative Catalyst

Remember to touch base with them when and as you apply their advice. Again, a line or two telling them, "I thought of last month's conversation the other day when I..." Let them know you aren't a one-shot deal.

Tell them if you can ever be of assistance to them or someone they know that you are always available.

Keep them posted on where you are. You never know the ramifications of the impression you made; if it feels right, keep them apprised of your progress.

Do not drop from view. Silence is just plain rude.

That being said, don't pester or overwhelm. Don't communicate without reason. Have substance in all your communication.

When you ask for information or support, acknowledge receipt. Don't put anyone in the position of asking if you received something. A simple "Got it, thanks" will do the trick.

"NRN" means "No Reply Necessary." A very handy "gift" when touching base with a mentor or resource. You're sending this person an update or acknowledgment; be sure they don't feel obligated to respond each time. Don't add to their workload—add to their sense of good investment in you.

Emails should be professional. Always address them by their name and use complete sentences. Yikes.

And in case this isn't obvious to you: Don't use TweetText in professional communications. No "how R U 2day?" Just don't.

Courtesy

Do not let communications rest idle for too long. If you're busy, swamped, or simply do not have time to give something the attention it requires, send a note acknowledging that and let the sender know they are on your radar and will get a response. You can hold your breath for the time it takes to write, "Am crazy busy, but will give this the time it deserves in a few days. Talk soon, Self." Pay attention to that; it pays off.

I have found that if I leave emails representing tasks I need to complete or obligations to fulfill in my inbox, that serves as a powerful "to do" tool for me. If I've told someone I'll get back to them, I leave that in my inbox so as to keep it in front of me. As that inbox begins to hover around sixty "read" messages, I know I'd better make time to address it. For me, it's a matter of integrity and professionalism.

If it's something you don't want to do or someone you'd rather avoid (we all have those and we've all done it), I feel quite strongly that we deal with these things respectfully. No human being should be ignored, ever. I say "hello" to panhandlers on the street, even when I don't give them money. Anyone who sends me an email is worth at least that much respect.

Just as space fills a vacuum, fiction can fill the void of silence, and that fiction is usually far more destructive than the truth. Don't make people wonder and fabricate possible reasons for your silence. If you've changed your mind on something, if deadlines or circumstances have changed, just let anyone waiting on you know.

Without delay.

Anyone who's ever waited for a phone call after a first date knows how slowly time can pass. Responding or addressing such things with alacrity removes doubt from the other end and takes the pressure off of you.

Respect

So that's what it's all about: Respect that grows from clean and sure communications. It doesn't take a lot of time; it does take some focused thought. Remember that the web is populated with millions of digital natives, but also by even more millions of digital immigrants. Immigrants arrive with preconceptions, habits, and opinions that may be of another era, but are just as valid to them as are the values, priorities, and habits of the natives.

If these differences are kept in mind as we all communicate with one another, if we maintain the discipline to remember the myriad approaches to communication, and that our goal is to be successful and productive in our communications across the lines of global culture and with those of, ahem, greater chronology, we will all be happier and likely more successful in our networking and career-building goals.

Know something about the others beforehand

Before meeting with someone new, whether a prospective client, employee, partner, investor, resource, or vendor, Google 'em. Do your research. There is a certain demographic that already knows this. I am regularly surprised, though, at the number of professionals who blithely make no use of this easily accessible, richly informative tool.

Countless are the times I've shown up for a first meeting, sometimes scheduled weeks in advance, and been asked about my background by someone who should already know as much about me as I know about them. Before sitting down across a table or desk from someone, know as much as you can about who they are and what they've done, especially in a professional context. This is simple stuff.

When I discover that the person with whom I'm meeting has not taken even a few moments to do such research, whether they are a potential employee or potential client, I am compelled to take another look at whether or not I even want that individual as a partner, teammate, or client. The ramifications of not performing a little background work are, frankly, profound, revealing, and often critical...and could adversely affect a potential working relationship.

Laziness, ignorance, fear of the internet, whatever the cause, the reticence to embrace and access the tools of the web indicates what it indicates; it's a big, red flag in every respect. Keeping abreast and conversant in the rapidly-evolving platforms of social media, research tools, communications platforms, and so on is critical for survival in business, especially in the business of experience creation and production. Eschew it and risk your very livelihood. Eschew it for long and the task can seem insurmountable.

Believe me, as decision makers grow younger, knee-jerk evaluations are made on what may seem insignificant or incidental to you, but are indicative of a relevant savviness—or lack thereof—that could easily cost one a gig or a client.

Creative Catalyst

Speaking of seemingly unimportant details, your email address can say enough to remove you from consideration. In an era when a personal or professional domain name costs only a few dollars and takes less than five minutes to set up, a Hotmail, Yahoo, or (ancient) AOL email address speaks of irrelevance and datedness before they even get to meet you. Your professional appearance is crucial, so make the effort.

Digital note-taking

It's cool and it's green to take notes on an electronic device. It offers lots of productive advantages. But, here's a distinctive nuance: It's one thing to take notes on your iPad during a meeting. People see what you are doing and tend to accept it. While keystroke tapping may irritate folks, using a laptop seems to be generally accepted. Keep your eye on the demographics (and politics!).

Taking notes on your phone, though, is likely to elicit a different reaction (again, depending on the people you're working with). Why? Because it looks as though you are texting.

Optics, everyone!

My suggestion is, in the absence of an iPad, paper is probably the best option for taking notes in most contexts. That being said, if you work in a corporate culture built of digital natives, then blend in and use your devices. Just know your audience...and know yourself!

It's actually possible that you might get more from the meeting by simply listening. Maybe don't take notes at all, or just jot a few keywords to trigger your memory later.

"Niche"

By the way...the word is pronounced "neesh." Sheesh...

Keeping agreements: Money and time

Money changes everything
Money, money changes everything
We think we know what we're doin'
That don't mean a thing
It's all in the past now
Money changes everything
They shake your hand and they smile
And they buy you a drink
They say we'll be your friends
We'll stick with you till the end
Ah but everybody's only
Looking out for themselves
And you say well who can you trust
I'll tell you it's just
Nobody else's money...

—Thomas Gray for Cyndi Lauper, 1983

Creative Catalyst

Building a team and a network of loyalty

When all is said and done, this is about respect.

You want to build a team, a network of people willing, if not downright looking forward to working with you, to join your team and create amazing things, and to return to your teams—time and again—to continue building great things?

Well then.

Respect them, and show them they are respected. Respect the deals that are made and never make anyone have to ask for their money.

It's key to remember that:

Putting people in a position to have to ask for their money, especially more than once, is demeaning to and disrespectful of them.

These people are working for you, they are not working for your client. When your client pays you is irrelevant to when you pay your people. This is a tough part of owning one's own business, though it remains a line not to be crossed.

Unless otherwise decided and contracted or agreed, all talent and show crew should walk away from the end of a project with a check in hand, fully paid.

A great opportunity for reinforcing the bond established through working together is to circulate among one's crew and team after the curtain has dropped and during load-out, handing these men and women their envelopes. Look them in the eye while personally thanking them for the gift of their efforts, skills, and talents in support of the team's collective vision. (In my case this process more often involves hugs and a few happy tears...but that's just me.)

As a freelancer back in my early days, I discovered that when I offered a 5% discount for being paid on the day of the event, the City of San Francisco would jump on it. I got paid the day of the event, saving me weeks of wondering when I'd see the money and keeping relationships solid for years of successive projects at and around city hall. Now, I did try that discount thing in Dubai, with the result that the client paid me a week late and still took the discount! So, that isn't necessarily a foolproof technique.

The point is that the actual payment of agreed upon fees directly affects the working relationship. Keep it clean and free of doubt; it will come back to you a thousandfold in respect, loyalty, and performance.

Time, deliverables, and deadlines

- Keep the agreement.
- Be on time.
- Deliver on time.
- Make the call on time.
- Do whatever you said you'd do on time...
- Avoid keeping people waiting, whether they are teammates, colleagues, or audience members.

As freelance, staff, vendor, or colleague, time agreements are of vital importance to the perceived integrity and dependability of you and the value of your word. Just as payment on time supports trust in professional relationships, so, too, do all time agreements serve to strengthen and support your integrity and bond with the team.

One person arriving ten minutes late to a meeting of six colleagues has effectively wasted sixty expensive minutes. One full hour of staff time. Lateness has a price; irrespective of the reason for it, there is rarely rationale.

The moment you know you're not going to arrive (pay, deliver) on time is the time to alert all concerned parties. Announcing one is late at the moment one is actually late is pointless; by then that secret is already out. By the way, this applies to any moment after people have begun to travel to gather for the meeting or function.

Meetings and professional commitments are not free-standing. People plan their days and workflow around meetings such that a cancellation even a few hours beforehand does not alleviate serious negative fallout. Companies staff up based on delivery schedules; failure to meet that schedule can cost significant amounts of money in lost or idle staff time (and overtime when compensating for your lateness). Be sensitive to the ramifications of failure to keep agreements, to keep one's word. Failure has consequences far beyond anything one might see or assume.

Don't commit unless you can do it, and don't fail to do it if you commit. Less than that is less than honorable. Respect your own word.

We are part of a team. Successive teams. We're part of a relationship or network of relationships that depend on trust and integrity to function fully well. From individuals to agencies to corporations, we are all bound to keep our word.

No context is too small to merit full commitment to integrity.

Your word matters.

Integrity is a constant discipline.

You must be committed to doing what you say, committed to your word always being dependable. Should something come up that causes a change in an agreement, integrity calls for immediate acknowledgment of that change.

There is no "play" in this; the keeping of your word is paramount. Acknowledging your mistakes and taking responsibility for resolution is an act of integrity. Realizing when you cannot keep your word and taking steps to acknowledge and rectify that is integrity. There is no escaping daily opportunities for embracing integrity. Not always easy, actions of integrity often result in stronger personal and professional relationships, healthier reputations, respect, and credibility granted from your peers.

In fields where bespoke teams are built for specific projects and productions, ultimately it's a person's reputation for dependability, integrity, and honor to be considered as someone who is reliable. When I know and recommend such people to other producers and directors, I describe the individual as, "He will hold onto the rope, as would a mountaineer...if he says he'll see to it, he'll see to it. You can depend on that."

Of course there are sudden, unique, even extreme times when you have to relinquish your responsibilities. These occasions generally involve death, deportation, incarceration, or some physical damage rendering one incapable of delivering.

There is a way to handle that:

Replace yourself...before you alert the client. Responsibility for duties undertaken, weeks or months before, cannot with integrity be handed back to the client for resolution when these are responsibilities you have embraced.

When you inform your client, have your qualified and vetted replacement briefed and ready. Your responsibility is to ensure a smooth transition and seeing that your position is covered.

Then there will be times when a better offer comes your way. That's an entirely different question.

Are you someone who will bail on the job to which you've guaranteed yourself?

Do you keep your current agreement and refer the new gig to someone else?

Do you hold onto the rope? Or do you bail?

This is a function of integrity, of the value of your word. At the end of the day, one must be complete with the reputation built by one's own actions.

Do you want to be known as excellent at what you do, a solid leader and team member, reliable and honest? Or...

Are you satisfied with being known as good at what you do, but might not see a project through if something better comes along?

There are plenty of individuals who have followed careers without always seeing projects through. I believe there are others better thought of, for whom their word is their bond.

Is short term financial gain more important than a reputation for reliability?

Once you begin to evaluate whether or not your word is worth keeping after the fact, you have departed the realm of integrity and crossed into another.

Just keep your word.

Take the long view

Scenario:

A few days ago, I was standing on a sidewalk in a local neighborhood, chatting with a friend and deciding where to go for dinner. As we were speaking, a police cruiser pulled up behind a vehicle that was double-parked in front of the row of restaurants where we were standing.

The officer didn't do anything; he just sat in his car. It looked as though he was catching up on paperwork, but of course I didn't know for sure. After about ten minutes, as my friend and I were crossing the street for our dinner destination, the pizza delivery guy responsible for the illegally parked vehicle showed up with his pizzas for delivery.

As he opened the hatch of his car, the officer lightly tapped on his horn and said, "Sir, your car is parked illegally…"

Question: What did the pizza delivery guy do? Did he say…

"I'm sorry, officer, I didn't mean to take so much time picking up these pizzas. I won't do it again. Thank you!" …and drive away?

or…

"Geez man, cut me a break! I'm just trying to earn a living here, man. Why you pigs gotta harass me?"

Ready with your answer?

You got it: option B. (And those were his exact words.)

Whereupon the cop got out of his car, closed the door, leaned back in through the window to grab his ticket book, and began walking up the street toward the man of the rapidly cooling pizzas.

My sense is that had delivery guy gone for option A, no ticket would have been written. On the heels of "It's easier to apologize than to ask permission" comes "Weighing the value of making a point versus realizing one's goal."

Okay, delivery guy was out of line. Yet, even when a point you may wish to make is valid, even when you are right, it's never a bad idea to assess and be aware of the ramifications of taking a particular stand that might affect your project, production, or deadlines. Whether it's another town, another state, another country, or simply another union leader, it's best to keep your eye on the overall goal when negotiating your way to production.

When being treated disrespectfully or condescendingly, when some bureaucrat, official, or relative of the client is throwing weight around or simply being obstructive, remember that this is most likely not personal...this person probably treats everyone this way.

So, the choice is:

To attempt enlightening this person about the waste that negativity and obstructionism engenders to the value of you and your team and the importance of your own priorities and deadlines...and fail. Or...

To be aware of all those things, but keep them to yourself and find the best way to most easily navigate your path to successful production. Sometimes this means acquiescing to what you may believe is beneath you or acceding to some requirement that seems ridiculous. (I say "seems," as you may not have all the pertinent facts). After all, who's gonna know and what's it gonna matter? Frankly, when giving in a little results in a show going up on time and coming in under budget, who's gonna care that you had an obsequious moment or two while ensuring that success?

Fortunately, as a Westerner I am not as culture-bound to the concept of saving face. But having the sensitivity to that very powerful cultural dynamic has more than once informed my own actions in the face of what may seem ridiculous. Giving the guy across the table the sense that he has won something can only help you down the line. It's not personal to you, but it may be very personal to your obstructor.

Have a slow fuse and take your time reacting or responding. Consider all variables and possible results and take the path of least resistance and best possible outcome. Save the sarcasm and vitriol for the cast party or an illustrative anecdote in a future conference presentation. Or write your own book. Avoid losing by winning.

15

A Culture of
Mentorship

Millennial has become a non-generational way of thinking...one which many older people have had trouble understanding and appreciating. No longer a word applying to a single generation, this point of view pervades successive generations and has become embraced upwards through the osmosis of collaboration.

In attempting to recognize where we are along the spectrum of cultural evolution, the fact is that at this moment the two largest factions in the U.S. workforce are boomers and millennials. The balance is shifting quickly, though. Coming up are generations of individuals who think differently, have different sets of values and aspirations, and who need the knowledge and mentorship represented in the rapidly shrinking numbers of boomers for effective institutional, intergenerational knowledge transfer in any industry.

A presentation was made at a recent industry panel discussion on the changing composition of the workforce, exploring adjustments to methodologies, mindsets, and existing corporate cultures. These are essential to success in embracing new demographics that have new or different ways of thinking than has been standard operating procedure since the Industrial Age...or at least the '80s.

Millennial seems to have become a pejorative, negatively-laden word. No matter how the term is meant when used, it seems to carry a volatility and be met with defensiveness and even anger. (I don't recall any previous generational generalization being met with such antipathy—not X, not Y, not even *boomer*...a term not without its own corona of entitlement. Yet that label never seemed to inspire such ire as does the "M"

234

word.) I'd like to find another word, but I doubt I ever will. For myself, I don't define *millennial* as a specific age group any longer.

As we mentioned in Chapter 8 on Leadership:

> **Typically applied as a label for a specific age demographic, its usage has evolved. If anything, *millennial* is a point of view, a way of seeing things, a combination of aspiration, inquisitiveness, and a sense of one's value (and perhaps a smidgeon of entitlement, here and there) that pervades vast segments of society and culture. It's now largely irrelevant to any particular age or generation and more broadly applies to exponentially greater segments of the professional workforce who plan to continue working for some time to come.**

In other words, pretty much anyone under 40 and many of the digital immigrants and industry elders has, by now and to at least some degree, adopted and embraced a more nimble, flexible way of thinking and communication...or is in the process thereof.

A few facts:

- By 2020 46% of the workforce in the US was predicted to be millennial. This number is greater than that of Boomers in the workforce.

- By 2025 more than half the workforce population will be reporting to someone younger than themselves.

- The smallest segment of the workforce with the greatest amount of industry and institutional knowledge has already crested sixty years of age. Far more active and healthy than the 60s of the '60s, this valuable population of elders wants to continue working, contributing, and sharing knowledge. We only have ten to fifteen years to see that knowledge and know-how shared; we must get on with it.

So here's the thing. Irrespective of one's perception, perspective, or impression of millennials the fact is inarguable these aspirational new thinkers are coming and must be welcomed and embraced. Whatever generalizations may be levied on this evolving workforce must be set aside with the larger view that we are bound to make this work.

And here's the other thing: Elders may need to learn to listen differently, better, more generously and acutely. This means shutting down preconception and silencing the voice in one's head, truly hearing the newcomer before deciding...

- when and how to share what knowledge.
- how open each might be to learning and collaboration.
- how best to relate, to establish positive, working relationships.

In his book, *Wisdom @ Work*, Chip Conley discusses the powerful synchronicity between the ways younger minds work in relationship to the minds of the elder generations. One is quick, reactive, and nimble while

Creative Catalyst

the other takes a more studied, responsive approach of consideration. The outcome of work produced by mixed-generation groups in collaboration, then, tends to be the most successful.

Road builders survey the topography before designing the road or laying pavement. It's the same with mentorship. Know with whom you are dealing, establish a respectful relationship before sharing knowledge, and be prepared to find new excitement or fulfillment in one's own learning from the person being mentored.

It truly is a two-way process. Active listening is critical to the building of a mutually respectful relationship. As we keep reminding ourselves throughout this book, leadership must be collaborative.

Mentors needed

Our industries are in the midst of a magnificent boom and associated crisis. It seems the world of themed entertainment and experience is at capacity in terms of experienced, skilled creative and production personnel to design, build, and open projects currently underway…and there are even more projects coming off the boards as this is written. Ground is well-broken on massive new theme parks all around the world. Beyond that are vast expansions of older parks, renovations of legacy installations, and dynamic ideation of properties and experiences we haven't yet seen.

It's a tsunami of abundance…

At any given time in some part of the world, an industry is scrambling to find experienced people to support projects currently in planning or already in progress.

At the same time, there are classes and masses of smart, talented, and aspirational young people coming out of design schools, universities, technical schools, and basements who possess the "book learnin'," the valuable objective knowledge and the passion that is going to drive entertainment and experience—and all business and culture—into the future.

These two rivers of project and resource are flowing together at a moment of synchronicity that stands to greatly benefit our industries and very likely completely evolve the way things are designed, done, sold, and experienced for the next few decades.

Thus, this convergence of harmonic opportunity…

There was a conversation some years back about the bestowing of titles that imply experience to those fresh out of school. This inflation has historically been seen as diminishing the title itself ("Creative Director," "Producer," and so on) while misleading the young person into delusions of grandeur.

Well…that's not gonna change. People are going to come out of school thinking they are ready for anything. In reality, this is not a problem; rather, it is a portentous opportunity…for all of us. The old-timers amongst our peers and colleagues in these industries need to embrace these new people, embrace their aspirations and ambitions, and support them in becoming who and what they see in themselves.

Creative Catalyst

Mentorship must be part of the program

Mentorship is no longer lunch-every-other-Thursday-with-one's-mentor as in the old days. The practice of mentoring should be embedded into every activity, every day, in the hallway, in the cafeteria, over coffee, at the water cooler, as well as in a boardroom. Any encounter with another might be an opportunity for mentoring. If a company or institution creates a culture of mentorship where anyone with a question or inquisitive look on their face can be met with "Got a question?" or "What's on your mind?" If any staff member, particularly someone new, is always and unfailingly met with openness and the intent to help incorporate that person into the fold and onto the team, the job is well on the way to being done.

This can transform "How we've done it..." into an answer, a precursor, a process of history rather than a defensive sword to be wielded. Here's how, here's why, here's what we got... Now, what do you see as a different solution...one that may perhaps be better, given what's happening now?

This requires a lot of ego-relinquishing from all parties interested in succeeding in the realization of personal or professional vision. It is also going to require a practice of assumption exploration and ongoing relinquishing of that assumption. That "kid" across the table might actually know some stuff, as might the white-haired geezer with the limp who at first glance looks like someone ready to retire.

So, embrace the new crop. Get to really know them. See them as equals in as many ways as you can and work on those relationships. If such an attitude can become woven into the culture of a company, organization, or project, productivity will increase and morale can skyrocket.

Creating a culture of mentorship is crucial in any context, where everyone coming through the door is valued for what each brings to the table. Combining institutional knowledge from the elders and new cultural, contextual knowledge from the fresher faces in the room seems the most positive, most potentially productive road to travel.

Share the glow

Along with this comes the invaluable opportunity to share with those who are new the incomparable sense of accomplishment when one has put in the work and effort over a significant amount of time to bring a project to conclusion or a program to life.

In a world filled with swipes, clicks, and likes, to discover the rewards of being totally immersed in the arduous work involved to reach ultimate accomplishment is a treasure to be shared. Perhaps you can approach the shepherding through the culture in such a way as to see the manifestation of intrigue as the delving-in begins, then witness the deep-seated excitement and visible thrill of accomplishment as success is realized.

16

Case Studies

et's see how all of this stacks up in practice. I've selected a few shows to critique, only one of which was an event I created. For the ones I had nothing to do with, I am unaware of the basis or rationale behind their decisions. I don't know the budget constraints and the ramifications those may have carried, nor any demands from the client. I don't know what edicts came out of some oversight, sponsor committee, or major donor's insistence.

I do know that quite often in these contexts there are many powers involved that can obstruct, circumvent, and derail even the best of creative concepts and production decisions. Creators do what they can, even though it doesn't always (ever?) turn out entirely as they envisioned.

With that in mind, I'm simply evaluating these shows from my own personal experience, from what I saw. My intent is not to insult or harm; if anything, I commiserate, having been forced to yield to similar pressures more than once. So, I feel the pain. That said, I also hold nothing back!

Reimagining tradition

What is one of our favorite parts of the Opening Ceremonies of the Olympic Games? Seeing our country's team enter the stadium in the Parade of Nations.

What is one of our least favorite parts of the Opening Ceremonies of the Olympic Games? Probably watching *every single team* of the Parade of Nations enter the stadium.

It's a part of the program that is both highly anticipated and deeply dreaded—thousands of athletes parading into the stadium, one after the other, encircling the stadium before taking their seats for the remainder of the ceremonies.

Two hours? Two-and-a-half? More...?

For the 1994 Gay Games Opening Ceremonies in New York City ("Unity '94"), rather than having the procession encircle the field, we had the Parade of Athletes march right down the center of Columbia University's Wien Stadium, north to south. Then, as each arrived at the south goalposts, teams would alternate turning right or left, circling back to take their seats at the edge of the field.

Spectators got to see their team enter and parade down the field, then half the audience got a second closer look as the athletes passed closer. We got 12,000 athletes into the stadium and seated in a record 75 minutes.

Twelve years later in 2006, we had the chance to do even better with the Opening Ceremonies at Chicago's Soldier Field.

These Olympic-style sports stadium ceremonies have the potential to be magnificent, moving, powerful spectacles of the highest, most resonant and exhilarating order. On the other hand, they also have the propensity to be cumbersome, protracted, over-speeched, and boring.

While we were intent on moving things along, we kept at the forefront of our minds the fact that these ceremonies are for and about the athletes. They are both the focus and the stars of the event, as well as being entitled to fully enjoy their presence and participation in such a ceremony. So, our perspective was that the Procession of the Athletes had to take place as near to the very first moment of the ceremonies as possible.

How to do that and do it both efficiently and effectively without shortchanging the athletes, while creating an indelible moment in the process?

There was no rehearsal time. Most of the athletes arrived in town the day before the opening ceremonies, some that same day. This meant anything done must be well conceived, well planned, fully thought through, and staffed for successful execution. We had an extremely tight budget with a small army of committed, intelligent volunteers and a darn good idea.

So, here's how it played out...

A forty-yard wide stage was built across the entire north end zone of the field. Across the broad hundred yard expanse of the field, in the south end zone, the unlit cauldron awaited the athletes, the ceremonies, and the ceremonial lighting.

The teams, rather than entering the stadium in columns to parade around the track, entered shoulder-to-shoulder in rows up to forty yards each. Bursting through a slit-mylar curtain, each team was revealed to the audience in total, all at once. (Though there were some teams so large they took several rows to fully enter).

At the moment of entry, the eyes of every person in the stadium were on that team—I dare say significantly more so than at any time after the first team enters in

the traditional staging of the Parade of Nations. Each team had that moment when all eyes were on them. The spotlight was all theirs.

Then, successively, each team moved forward onto the field and continued to parade across toward the other end, waving and cheering, owning the field. As the teams reached the far end, they effectively filled the space Tetris-style.

The only thing the athletes knew in advance was that they would be handed a light on a lanyard as they arrived on the field and that they would be participating in a "light stunt" at the close of the Processional and the Administering of the Oath to the athletes. They did not know what that stunt would be, nor did the audience have any inkling that there would even be a stunt. The athletes were told to "light up" the moment the house went dark.

So, as they arrived at their positions they were met by one of six teams of volunteers, each distributing a different colored light. Each column of athletes had a specific color and was guided by barely visible hand-held rope barriers that unfurled as the athletes gathered, masking their presence. This way, the lights were kept separate so as to be discerned as panels when they were activated on cue.

The procession of more than 11,000 athletes was completed in 47 minutes—an "Olympic" record by at least half.

The procession began before the sun started to set. The stadium lights were already on so that darkness would be a surprise when they were extinguished. The athletes entered, gathered, were given their LEDs, and then led in the Athlete's Oath by sports icon Dave Kopay.

As the last words of the Athlete's Oath were given voice…

"In these Games I have no rivals, only comrades in Unity…"

The house went dark, the LED lights came on, and the audience went nuts as a football field-sized, electronic Pride Flag appeared before them, filling the floor of the stadium. It was awesome in the truest sense of the word.

The explosion of exhilaration and energy was almost overwhelming. The surprise of the audience as they saw what was before them elicited to-their-feet cheering. Then, as that first roar began to peak, the eyes of the athletes on the field could see via the IMAG screens what they had created and went even wilder with that realization. This, quite literally, stopped the show.

As though that weren't enough, as the athletes realized what they'd made, they began to swirl their lanyards. I wish I could say that this had been envisioned, but the lanyards were part of planning for so many athletes who would be in sports gear, possibly pocketless.

When they began swirling the lights, it was breathtaking, as though the stadium were awash in living, liquid light. My production manager and I ran from the booth to the field in order to stand in it, walk through it, to cheer and hug other athletes and to immerse ourselves in the most immersive of spectacles I'd experienced.

In retrospect, these are excellent examples of some of the things I've been talking about:

1. Liberating preconception and comfortable disorientation with the reconfiguring of the procession.
2. Successive revelation of the athletes as they entered, with the filling of the field, and finally with the reveal of the flag first to the audience, then to the athletes.

So powerful, the experience. So proud to have been successful. So grateful for that memory.

London Olympics Opening Ceremony

Well done, I'd say. Very well done—at least at the time.

My experience of the London Opening Ceremonies was, of course, limited to what I was able to glean through the NBC broadcast in the U.S., interrupted as it was by countless commercial breaks and the distracting and inane prattling of the on-camera hosts. Regrettably, at one point NBC cut away from the entire performance of the reverential and moving Tribute to Terror Victims for an interview of U.S. swimmer Michael Phelps. The network had decided that it was inappropriate for American audiences.

I'll start with my initial impressions immediately after the event, then share what I was thinking a week later, after I had more information on hand and the whole thing had sunk in a bit.

Creative Catalyst

Overall impression

The implied mandate or challenge, of course, was to somehow beat the unbeatable. "How are they going to beat Beijing?" That four-year conversation found common ground in conjecture that London would "have to go in a different direction," and in a different direction Danny Boyle did go!

Beautifully.

Compared to Beijing's awesome spectacle, I found the London ceremonial experience to be magnificently personal. Beijing's production featured one jaw-dropping moment after another, virtually incredible displays of technology with massive, choreographed stunts and effects performed with precision by thousands of essentially "invisible" performers.

Time and again, four years ago we'd all be asking "HOW did they do THAT?" It was truly awesome what the producers were able to accomplish. The production was slick, timed to the millisecond, massive, heavy with technology, and it projected an aggressive pride in accomplishment for the PRC...and rightly so.

In London's ceremony, on the other hand, one could see every single performer. Nothing was hidden—it was all there. The magic was in...here it comes...the subliminal engagement of the audience in offering them the opportunity to personally involve themselves in the creation of their own experience.

What was slick and clean and impressively sterile in Beijing was, in London, broad and expansive and a little cluttered...and almost (almost!) messy...and very deeply human.

What I liked

The drums. From the beginning, Boyle filled that stadium with percussion. Drums—the first, most primitive of musical instruments and the one that shakes people right to their bones. Drums: GREAT call. They showed up in many forms and different contexts and kept the audience resonating, thus open to the stories that were being told on a subconscious level. Primal.

The intense experience of percussion actually stimulates the most primal part of the brain and our ancestral wiring. There is no thinking at all involved in appreciating percussion, as we communicated with drums even before there was fire. Opening the show with drums and interweaving them throughout keeps the right brain actively alive and open for more.

The LED beds and bedsheets: just a cool effect. I want to use it, somewhere.

The doves. I thought the doves were brilliant. Combining the symbol of peace so evocatively with the art, discipline, and craft of cycling, something so intrinsically British, had to have brought a gasp to the throats of the audience in the stadium. From their entrance until the final "ET"-esque flight into the sky, these doves brought a magic into the space that was ethereal...something to make the audience reach.

This was another excellent example of subliminal engagement. Much as I've cited Julie Taymor's ancient costume design inspiration for The Lion King, the audience can see and appreciate all the pieces they see before their imaginations kick in and take them beyond what lies before them. Wonderful.

The set. At first it seemed a little Middle Earth-like. But as it became populated I began to appreciate what we were being given. Again, spectacle on a human scale. As the set evolved, through a transition that was primarily of the lowest tech possible—actual human beings, it became more and more familiar and impressive.

It was theatrical. Essentially, the entire production was presented theatrically, and it worked.

The flame entering the stadium. From the moment Steven Redgrave took the flame from David Beckham and the pyro fountains went off behind him, I was moved. The dark run to the stadium, the honor guard of 500 construction workers, the youthful representatives of the future of sport in the UK…face to face, generation to generation. This was powerful imagery.

The flame circling the stadium. Watching those kids run the track, beatific smiles on their faces as they appreciated where they were, had me close to openly weeping. This is why I watch these things in private.

The fluid ease with which they passed the torch from one to the other with successive legs of the circuit was symbolic of teamsmanship, a camaraderie that I'd like to think is more predominant in the next few generations than I may have seen in my own. It was powerful.

The lighting and the cauldron. Inspired. Inspired. Inspired.

There was a little successive revelation combined with liberation from preconception—and a touch of OMG—as we were able to realize that those things we saw being carried in with the athletes were part of something bigger…as in the biggest part of the ceremony.

There have been bigger and more awesome cauldron lightings. For me, Barcelona will ever remain the most authentic, human achievement in this context. The aim of Antonio Rebollo had to be perfect and true; there was no second shot. It was a breathtaking moment. Beyond that, the lightings of several more recent ceremonies have been spectacular with pyrotechnics coming from everywhere, leaving the audience agape with the sheer charge and energy. Wonderful, big, impressive...

But London 2012 did something viscerally metaphorical. This happened gently and slowly, paced almost organically, for us to realize piece by piece as the shells came alight, that there may be more before us than meets the eye. Moving slowly, much as might the coming together of nations and people, the shells rose on their pylons to gather on high and take the shape of the Olympic cauldron—reflecting the gathering of nations for one purpose that is the Olympics.

And, rather than being high above the field, towering over the city, it is at the heart of the field of play in the center of the stadium. Embraced by the surrounding competitors and nations.

Pretty cool.

The hands-free lighting stunts. What a gift to the audience to relieve them of physical duties during the show. Instead, LED screens were placed at each seat to do that work for them. The effect, on television, was exceptional, reflecting or magnifying what was taking place on the field. I've no idea how it felt to be sitting among that, whether it was or wasn't distracting. But it sure looked good for the show.

Creative Catalyst

What I'm not so sure about

All that intricate choreography on a field, so far away. From the Industrial Revolution segment onward, there was some pretty intimate storytelling going on all over that field. Did that read? Was it necessary to have IMAG (image magnification on screens) in order to fully appreciate what was taking place on the field? Were that the case, would that not split focus between field and screen? My own practice is to keep cameras off the field and never allow them between audience and experience.

Length of each segment. I thought they went on a bit long for my taste. That being said, there was so much going on, on the field, that perhaps the dance numbers had to go on a bit for the audience to take it all in. I suppose one had to be there.

Parade of Nations. Didn't this used to be a tad more formal, perhaps a bit regimented? All ceremonial-like with people in lines and rows with pomp and circumstance? It seems that only a few small African nations treat this moment with deep respect and reverence, while the Caucasians are all about the spotlight and being just a little self-absorbed. It's as though the athletes used to be moved and thrilled to be marching into the stadium, and now they are thrilled and pleased to be marching into the stadium "...so that everyone can see ME!"

I like ceremony, and I'm a tad disappointed to see this degeneration of formality. At the same time, they sure do look happy. But it's still TOO LONG!

Camera work. It seemed that a lot depended on camera work—close ups and cutaways and, during the child and adolescent segments, on-screen close ups and pop-ups.

Ironically this worked great on television, but I can't imagine it working in the stadium without people having to look at the IMAG screens. (Unless that was a function of the at-seat screens in the stadium. While that would still split the focus, it might minimize the dissonance.)

Rowan Atkinson and the London Philharmonic. Didn't get that one at all. But then, I am not British. I know the guy's loved. On the other hand, I kept thinking during that segment what a bunch of good-natured sports the London Philharmonic musicians must be—to be playing at the Olympic ceremonies and be completely upstaged by a comic and a film clip. So, hey—I guess it worked!

Finally...

Am I missing something? When the teen girl lost her phone and the boy found it, and then called to tell her, on what device did she answer?

I was wowed and awed by the spectacle of Beijing; the net effect there was of being impressed by technological and logistical prowess. With London, I am moved and touched by the humanity and intimacy, the personal-ness of what was delivered. It evoked feelings and made us embrace them in order to appreciate what we were seeing. It engaged the audience with the familiar, then took us further. Very well done.

...and, the British are, by all I know and can see, very good sports about themselves.

Creative Catalyst

After further consideration and a week of rumination, however...

During the week after the event, I was able to learn more about how the event transpired for those in the venue. I also discovered that I'd made two egregious errors in my first-pass analysis of the work:

1. I missed the first of my own Tenets of Experience Creation; that being Exploration of Assumption. Neglecting to consider any assumptions I was making, I leaned toward acceptance of some components of show and approaches to the storytelling that were more than ill-advised...they were downright misguided, results of poor judgment and myopic decision-making.

2. I allowed myself to be swayed and become emotionally engaged by the "fact" of some of the components, despite the distracting presentation of them.

Now that being said, there is nothing wrong with being moved by these ceremonies, even as they were presented. Quite the contrary, simply being moved is really one of the points of such ceremonies and spectacle. Many of the components and approaches to which I referred to as perplexing me were, upon further exploration, actually poorly-informed miscalculations and poorly-conceived approaches.

On the positive side, I liked what I liked and still like those few, profound components I experienced. I was moved by the presence of the athletes and the Fact of the Moment, though I now see—what was made quite obvious with input from my peers—that I brought a lot of myself to my experience of the event, seeing it through my filter of evocation.

Evocation is one of the most powerful forms of storytelling. Touching the memories and making emotional connections within each audience member is, ultimately, crucial to effective storytelling...from the historical to the fantastic, it's gotta connect.

I failed to maintain my objectivity and to experience the ceremonies with the global purpose in mind in lieu of indulging in my own sentimentality. A wonderful luxury, and not my purpose in this context. After much impassioned conversation shared in emails and phone calls, I was able to recalibrate and have my professional equilibrium restored.

What has come to light, for me, is the extent to which this production was conceived and staged for a television audience. What I accepted, soft-pedaled, as irregularities and distractions were, ultimately, the result of intentional planning. The show was choreographed primarily to be experienced onscreen. Some of the dance numbers were so intricately intimate in their staging as to be lost to those in the stadium.

Broadening the perspective, the importance people place on these ceremonies requires them to be far greater than the sum of their successive parts. The world seeks evocative magnitude and did not get it.

Not good.

Some specifics:

First and foremost, what was missing was sweep and scope, a sense of momentum and global history on a grand scale. Most of the ceremony was insular and self-referential to Britain; I don't recall seeing much presentation of a global perspective in the ceremonies, and virtually no reference to or evocation of the Olympic heritage beyond the Parade of Nations.

The metaphor of the Forging of the Olympic Rings was brilliantly launched and executed. A powerful, dynamic, and energetic image that didn't go anywhere.

Sadly lost, especially in the stadium, was the metaphor of the cauldron. Of those to whom I've spoken who were in the stadium, none were even aware of the copper "shells" being carried at the head of each delegation, and no one saw them being placed in the ground. No foreshadowing, no explanation, no awareness. My contacts each learned of the connection when watching the recorded broadcast afterwards.

That could have been presented so much better, making more of a visual point of each one as it was carried in, along with the gathering of them into the cauldron if that were possible.

We who had close-up views and ongoing (sometimes relentless) television commentary became aware of the genesis of the cauldron just before ignition. It was a magnificent metaphor, the gathering of nations to rise and ignite the Olympic flame. Unfortunately, that deep, human, most meaningful nuance was not communicated to the audience in the stadium...and only barely so to the global audience...at least that in the U.S.

Missteps among the trivial and picayune would include:

DIVIDING THE FOCUS OF THE AUDIENCE. This is anathema in live spectacle. The intentional need for video screens in order to appreciate the story being told (when there was a story), keeps the left brain distractingly engaged while the audience seeks to put the components together and make sense of the experiential narrative. This diminishes the experience. To truly connect and evoke, the story must be delivered via the right brain, keeping the analytical left brain dormant and quiet.

TELLING STORIES NOT GERMANE TO THE REST OF THE WORLD. Once the "narrative" launched into national health care, it became irrelevant to most other countries. We get that the Brits are proud of this system, and it's a good one...a solid success story. What is this to be telling the populations of countries that do not have it? How is it relevant to the rest of the world during the Olympics?

THE PARADE OF NATIONS. I have never understood why the athletes don't enter the stadium immediately after the opening of the Ceremony. The athletes are the most important part of that night as well as the entire Olympics; not only are they a highlight of the "show," they ARE the spectacle, the raison d'ceremony. I see no reason they should miss a moment of the night. This is not specific to London 2012, though this was the least ceremonial of an entrance I've seen. I believe the athletes should enter first and be the only focus of the stadium for that (albeit protracted) moment.

Creative Catalyst

FAR TOO MUCH FREE-STANDING VIDEO. (Bond & Her Majesty.) Okay, fine, have your fun. Still, that bit might have played better at closing, but it did communicate the full support of the Regent. Beyond that, the filming of everything from choirs to the torch jetting down the Thames (part of which was obviously pre-recorded) not only effectively divides focus, but more importantly removes the minds and imaginations of the audience from what is before them in the stadium.

As I mentioned, what I liked up front, I still like. In taking a breath, putting my inner pollyanna to bed and taking an experiential storyteller's look at the show, I am obligated to take this bolder stance in what perplexed me. A wonderful experience, a nice job, yet I believe the London ceremony fell far short of meeting its purpose and mandate.

It is not unheard of for audiences, having spent great amounts of money for something hyped beyond measure, to convince themselves that what they experienced was fantastic and surpassed all expectation. We've seen it on Broadway, we've seen it in theme parks, we've seen it in stadia.

The London ceremonies, in the context of a television spectacular celebrating Britain, were good; there were some wonderful, powerful moments. Some parts were excitingly imaginative, profoundly well-conceived and staged; some other parts were quite the opposite. They were big and good and fun...a fine television show.

As a live experience, not so much.

Not quite Olympian.

What I'm looking for

Audience expectation is limited by what they believe is possible. It is our responsibility, as creators of experience, to take them where they do not expect to go.

Whenever I'm looking forward to an experience event, there are some leading questions and criteria on my mind. Irrespective of the subjectivity of the creative aspects, the execution of the narrative and ceremonial aspects of the event, show, or experience is my primary focus.

Does it make sense?

If there's a narrative, a storyline, or an arc to the experience, does it unfold with logic, invite suspension of disbelief, engage the audience in a way that it can be experienced—intimately and personally—at the same time as it is shared by the thousands? That, to me, is the key to truly compelling experience. It can be done for groups of two to 200,000 or more.

Is the experience seamless?

Do components flow from one into the other without explanation? Does it engage the audience?

Are the best seats in the house IN the house?

I believe that live, stadium, or destination-specific spectacle is best envisioned, designed, and created for the audience that is present. For full integrity, it is the audience on-site that should reap the potential rewards of a well-conceived and executed, emotionally connective, immersive experience.

Is the storytelling dependent on media and screens?

I have yet to see this done in a way that doesn't distract. In my experience, peripherally-projected video rarely fails to distract from a story—it splits the focus of the audience. (As compared to video that is woven into the storytelling and located within the physical space of the action.)

Meanwhile, I believe that it is literally impossible to recreate the full experience of a live spectacle with any camera. At best, the "audience at home" will gain only a sense of that which is taking place live. They can only appreciate; they cannot experience.

Given that, any attempts to bring the remote audience into the experience run the risk of obstructing or distracting from the experience and the entire thing will fall short of the intended goal. All one can do with cameras is offer glimpses of what is happening and to elicit feelings of "Wow, I sure wish I could be there…"

Thus the producer should shoot the experience from the point of view of the audience, sharing what can be shared rather than attempt to do the impossible, which degrades the experience of those present.

The wedding photographer backing himself up the aisle in front of the bride, barely avoiding bumping up against the wedding party. The gnat-like profusion of close-up cameras on a performing field during televised spectacle experiences. Such efforts are distracting and fruitless.

For my money, and especially with the quality and power of photographic equipment, there is never an excuse to have anything other than Show on the field or stage during a performance. Place cameras over-head, rigged and flown, locked down, or whatever it takes to capture the spectacle—not break it down into micro-components.

An example from my own experience

Chicago, 2006 Gay Games Opening Ceremonies. The 11,000 athletes had just left the field after having taken the Oath of the Athletes and creating a spectacular, full-field lighting stunt.

Now it was time for the oath to the officials. In stark contrast to the field full of athletes, the vision was for Billy Bean, the presenter of the oath, to walk from one end of the field to meet soccer star Saskia Webber, oath proxy, in the exact center of the stadium. This stark contrast between the crowd of participants and an expansive, empty field of play—of "battle"—with just the two standing in the center for the oath-taking was to be breathtaking and awesome.

And, it would have been.

Except for one, selfishly myopic photographer who wanted to get "the shot." Midway through the 90-sec-ond oath, he leapt over the wall on the sidelines of the field, ran to the center, crouched behind Saskia and began taking shots from every angle behind and around the two principals. He was a disorienting distraction to the two on the field, but more than that, what he managed to do was distract the 50,000 people in the stadium and become the show.

He took excellent pictures of something that no one else experienced. He shot two people on the field in

Creative Catalyst

close-up. What everyone SAW was three people. What was to have been formal and ceremonial became humorous and annoying, and what was remembered was the photographer (who, by the way, was ejected from the stadium without comprehending the reason) rather than these two sporting icons and their roles.

Videos from the event are available on my website and YouTube channel.

17

The Call

The goal was to tell a substantive, compelling story in an engaging way. The challenge was keeping a thousand people interested, entertained, receptive, and off their mobile devices through the program while hoping there would be minimal early departures from the event.

The occasion was the 30th anniversary recognition event for the San Francisco AIDS Foundation at the Regency Ballroom in San Francisco in June of 2012. The guarantee was "no speeches" and, other than an enthusiastically-received set of remarks by Democratic Leader Nancy Pelosi at the very start of the evening, that assurance was respected. All messaging was done theatrically in four six-to-eight minute vignettes that were spread over the first two hours of the three-hour event.

The concept was to articulate the chronological, socio-political, and emotional arcs of the AIDS epidemic of the past thirty years through these vignettes. Action took place on the proscenium stage, on two platform stages juxtaposed among the cocktail-sized tables in the room, and from the encircling overhead balcony.

The guests were provided only an address on a street adjacent to the theatre/ballroom where the event was to take place. Exiting their car or cab, they were directed to an alleyway where, as the corner was turned, they saw before them a classic red carpet lined with paparazzi…

Walking down the carpet and through a grungy, beat-up door under a fire escape, then up two flights of stairs (accommodations were made for those who needed to avoid stairs), the guests suddenly found themselves on stage in a nightclub setting. That entry path cleansed the palate of preconception and gave each audience a moment of awe. Very few had ever been on that stage and seen the room from that vantage point. A stairway then led them from center stage down to the main floor.

The room was set up as a club: heavy on small tables of varying shapes and heights, light on seating, heavy on a wide variety of easily-eaten food on small plates. All to keep people moving and comfortable and not stuck with nine others at a static dinner table for the entire night.

The strategy was to communicate through the first vignette that these would be short, intense, and impactful, sending the message that mobile devices and mouths would be pretty much closed during the performances. Talking and texting would be accommodated in the twenty to twenty-five minutes between acts.

It worked.

The first act, "Discovery," was so powerfully delivered that not one screen was lifted from a pocket. Watching from the rear as I was calling the show, I could see no devices raised. We had 'em, and this dynamic was repeated in each of the ensuing three acts: "Triage," "Defiance," and "Empowerment."

This continued all the way to the end.

After the intensity of the first act the lights faded before each successive one, and the audience—having been shown that the interruption would be brief, intense, and worth watching—would simply fall silent and turn to the stage. Phones set down, each person gave themselves over to the show.

Script – "The Call"

Here are the scripts for the experience. Performed by actors on loan from ACT on the stage, platforms, and balcony, and framed with video codas, attention-grabbing musical performance, and a soloist, the story was compellingly told and received with everything from tears to thunderous applause.

Act I – Discovery

Just as the guests are settling into the party, first drinks in hand and buffet stations inspected and selected, suddenly disco music from the 70s (Donna Summer's "I Feel Love") bursts from the speakers. The lighting goes to fabulous, spotlights ballyhoo, and colors flash everywhere as the encircling balcony and free-standing platforms are filled with flaggers. We are at The Saint or Trocadero, and the year is 1981 or 1982…

For a full minute the audience is immersed in fantastic, frenetic, kinetic nostalgia, smiling at the blurred memories of dancing 'til dawn in self-actualized celebration of liberation and freedom…

The music suddenly comes to a stop. The upper reaches of the ballroom go dark as the lights move across the audience to focus on the stage. There, standing in a column of light is the boy, quiet. We hear the ringing of a telephone through the receiver of a landline phone of the late '70s…

Creative Catalyst

Mom:
Hello…?

Boy:
Hello, Mom? It's me.

Mom:
So I see. Where are you? Are you coming home?

Boy:
I'm not coming home, Mom; I live in San Francisco.
For now, anyway…

Would you put Dad on the extension, please? I have
something I want to tell you both.

Mom:
I think we already know anything you could tell us by
now…

Boy:
Actually, Mom, I don't think you know this. Please get
Dad on the line…

Mom (hollers to Dad):
Pappa, Honey, get on the extension. Our son has
something he wants to tell us.

Dad:
Hey, kid, how's it going out there in…California?

Boy:
Hey, Dad. Mom.

So, listen. How are you guys doing out there? Has it
snowed yet? The weather here is always so mild…
well, except in the summer, when it gets cold and
foggy…(weak laugh)… I miss you guys. Mom, I miss

your cooking. I've lost some weight, (takes a breath) recently, and sure could go for some of your mashed potatoes and gravy...

(uncomfortable silence)

Mom:
Son, we haven't heard from you in months, and this is what you call to talk about? Weather and food?

Boy:
No. No, that's not what I wanted to talk about. I just think about you a lot, recently, and I wanted...Well, I need to tell you some things, some stuff I've been keeping to myself for a long time, some stuff that's a little newer...

Dad:
Did you lose your job, son? Are you okay? Do you need money?

Mom:
He's a big boy, Pappa, he can take care of himself. After all, he moved clear to California to be on his own, didn't he...?

Dad:
Mamma...

Boy:
Dad, it's all right. I still have a job.

So, here's the thing. I know how upset you were when I didn't propose to Susie, and that you've never been happy about me moving away. I just had to get to a bigger place.

I never felt right in our town. I never fit, and I knew

if I came someplace like San Francisco, I might fit in
better, meet more people....like...me...

Mom/Dad:
(quietly) like you...?

Boy:
So, the first thing I need to tell you is that I'm Gay.
I've known it forever, it feels like. I kept hoping that
maybe I'd grow...that I'd...But it never...

Dad:
We know, son. We knew, didn't we, Momma...?

(silence)

Boy:
I thought you might, but I was afraid to bring it up. I
didn't want to disappoint you. I know you had plans...

Dad:
You didn't dis...

Boy:
(interrupting) There's more, Dad. Mom.

Mom:
(almost coldly, stoic) What is it?

Boy:
Well, I mentioned I've lost some weight. Actually, I've
lost a lot of weight, sorta fast. I'm sick.

Mom:
(very stoically, with bitterness) What is it? A flu?
Pneumonia? I knew all that fog...

Boy:
It's not the flu, Mom. I don't know what it is. There's a lot of confusion about what's going on, and a lot of guys are getting sick...very sick...very fast. No one is sure where it's coming from, but other guys like me are getting it, all over the place...guys like me...It's scary...I'm scared, a little...

Dad:
(bravely) What are your symptoms, Son? Are you coughing? What...?

Mom:
Do you have a fever?

Boy:
That's what's so scary. At first, I was just so tired... just climbing stairs was wearing me out for no reason. Then, about two weeks ago, these spots started showing up on my legs; then, last week, there were a couple on my chest....

(silence)

Then, this morning as I was shaving, I found one on my cheek. (he chokes a little) ...on my face, Mom! My face...

Dad:
(quietly) What does your doctor say? Are you taking anything? What's your treatment?

Mom:
What do these spots look like? What's on your face?

Boy:
That's just it; nobody knows what to do about it.

There seems to be no medicine for this. These spots...
they look like big brown amoebas made of the same
stuff as a mole or a dark freckle...they're ugly...

Mom:
Are you in pain, Honey? How did you get this?

Boy:
No one seems to really know where it comes from,
but it's hitting all my friends. Lots of guys I know or
used to see around just seem to be disappearing.
First they get tired like I did, then they lose a lot of
weight, then you just don't see them anymore...

(silence)

They just...disappear...My friends...disappearing...

Mom:
Well. Perhaps if you hadn't...

Dad:
(cuts her off) We're coming out there, son.

Mom:
We are...?

Dad:
Yes, we are. We'll make arrangements to get out there,
next week. You sure you don't need any money?

Mom:
Can you get the time off, Pappa?

Dad:
I can get the time off. We'll come out there. Anything
you want us to bring...?

Boy:
I don't need anything, Dad. I'd just like to see you...
Mom, would you make some mashed potatoes while
you're here...?

(fade out)

Act I Coda – Voice-over in the darkness

"His parents may have made it to San Francisco in time
to say 'goodbye' to their son, or perhaps not. In those
dark and confusing, early years it was often a matter of
only a few, short weeks between discovery, diagnosis,
and death. By the time one realized weight was dropping too fast, that the bruise was more than a bruise,
the disease was often in advanced stages. It was as
though a brutal, autumn wind swept through this city,
taking with it hundreds of young men and women, like
so many brittle leaves, week after month after year.

"Many parents, brothers and sisters, friends, rela-
tives rushed to San Francisco only to arrive too late.
Our community, seeking and finding no help from
elsewhere, was going to have to address this thing by
ourselves. And that, we did...

"Over those first few years San Francisco's response
for triage and caregiving, for succor and sustenance,
set the bar and became what the rest of the country
and now the world see as the model for communities to
deal with the myriad needs that appeared.

"Concurrently, we had to face and aggressively
enlighten a nation, striving to protect ourselves from
and eliminate an instantly inherent, blaming prejudice
coming even from government agencies and leadership.

Creative Catalyst

"What was happening was unprecedented, unfathom-
able, inexplicable—a swift-moving, deadly mystery that
was pulling our lives out from under us. A vale of tears
through which most all of us passed, perhaps not at the
same time, nor the same place, and all too often, alone.."

Act II – Triage

(Phone rings.) (Another phone rings, overlapping.)
(Then, another...)

(Louder ring as house lights begin to fade.)

(Then, two phones...then more, and more, until there
is a cacophony of phones ringing, louder and louder
until conversation can't compete. Concurrently and
in counterpoint, house lights fade to black.)

(Phones stop, suddenly. At the same time Volunteer,
in position on stage, is lit.)

Volunteer:
Hello. California AIDS Hotline. How can I help you?

Caller (Roger):
Is this an anonymous hotline?

Volunteer:
Yes. We are completely anonymous. We don't record
calls, we don't ask names...

In rapid succession:

Roger:
I think I'm sick. I think I have this thing...what is it
even called? GRID?

Rick:
I've lost so much weight in the last two weeks...

Pam:
I don't know how to say this...

Patrick:
I think I need to get tested...

Josh:
There's this mark on my arm.

Rick:
There's a mark on my leg.

Pam:
There's a mark on my stomach.

Roger:
There's a mark on my face.

Rick:
I don't want my doctor to know.

Patrick:
I don't want my parents to know.

Alex:
I can't tell my roommates.

Josh:
How can I tell my lover?

Pam:
What about my kids?

Roger:
If anyone in my church finds out...

Josh:
Is there someone I can talk to...?

Rick:
I hear there's a test to see if one has it. Is there a test? Do I have to give my name?

Pam:
I don't want to give my name to anyone.

Patrick:
How long til I get my results...?

Rick:
My boss saw the lesions on my arm, and now I don't have a job...

Josh:
I've been denied my Social Security...they just don't seem to know what's going on...

Roger:
I went to the Red Cross Blood Drive at work...

Josh:
They asked me how much sex I've had!

Rick:
Then, they told me they couldn't take my blood; they sent me away.

Patrick:
I was...embarrassed.

Roger:
Fired from my job...I can still work...is there a way to find work?

Josh:
I came home and all my stuff was on the street; my roommates have locked me out...

Pam:
I need help to keep my electricity.

Rick:
Where can I live? Is there someplace I can call to get help?

Pam:
I'm running out of money...

Roger:
I have no health insurance...

Patrick:
I can't pay my rent...

Pam:
I have a baby...what about nursing?

Roger:
I just read that the mayor has declared a state of emergency and endorsed needle exchange...

Rick:
I went to visit my friend in the hospital, and they made me put on a hazmat suit!

Patrick:
My lover is in the hospital, they won't let me see him; I'm not family!

Josh:
I'm afraid to leave my house!

Pam:
I'm pregnant...

Josh:
I can't stand for people to see me.

Rick:
Can you get it from kissing?

Roger:
Can you get it from shaking hands?

Pam:
Can you get it from a sneeze?

Rick:
Hello, I'm a physician, calling from Kentucky...I don't know where to get the information I need...Where might I learn about your needle exchange program?

Patrick:
My lover is sick. I wake up every morning afraid of what I might find. I need to talk to someone...

Roger:
Is there someone?

Pam:
I think my husband might be Gay...

Josh:
I don't have the energy to walk my dog. I feel sorry for her...

Roger:
I'm too tired to cook; besides, there's no food in the house, really...

Patrick:
I hear there's someone who delivers meals? Can I know who that is...?

Pam:
What can you tell me about Hospice care? I have a friend...

Rick:
My friend died.

Josh:
My friend died.

Patrick:
My friend died.

Roger:
My lover has died.

Pam:
My brother has died.

Patrick:
So many funerals.

Rick:
I want to scatter his ashes here in San Francisco...

Josh:
Is there someplace I can do that?

Roger:
He just loved it here...

Pam:
He's our president; he won't even say the word!

Creative Catalyst

In rapid succession:

Roger:
I live in the Castro

Josh:
West Hollywood

Rick:
Sunset

Patrick:
Yreka

Josh:
Richmond

Pam:
Fresno

Patrick:
The Mission

Roger:
Redding

Pam:
Potrero

Rick:
Ukiah

Roger:
The Marina

Josh:
Palm Springs

Rick:
Pacific Heights

Patrick:
San Jose

Josh:
The Haight

Pam:
Mill Valley

Patrick:
Daly City

Roger:
Davis

Pam:
Pacifica

Rick:
Napa

Roger:
Oakland

Josh:
Tracy

Rick:
Sacramento

Patrick:
Modesto

Pam:
Turlock

Roger:
San Diego

All:
Am I going to die?

Act II – Coda

"…It was out of the ashes, turmoil, confusion, and fear that the Gay and Lesbian community of San Francisco actually became community. As thousands of men became ill and died, thousands of women stepped in to care for them; where there had been schism grew a powerful bond.

"Dealing with a formless and formidable foe, we gathered to shelter, feed, and offer succor to those whose lives were disappearing before their own eyes and before ours.

"None of us had time to grieve…responding, racing, and reaching to catch and care for the fallen, one after another. Breathlessly poised and responsive to one another, we took care of one another.

"In taking care of ourselves, before this vicious and aggressive virus even had a name, we created a critical network of service organizations that grew and evolved, split and merged, addressing the needs as the needs grew and changed. Hospice to care for dying with no homes to embrace them, Project Open Hand to feed them, a Quilt to Remember even as we continued to die—alliances of men and women, friend and former

Creative Catalyst

foe, doctors and nurses, artists, therapists, brothers, sisters...

"A network of sustenance and advocacy that has continued to evolve to meet the needs of our community, led by what is now the San Francisco AIDS Foundation..."

(Spotlight up on house right platform)

Tim Hockenberry at keyboard, sings "Just Breathe."
(Pearl Jam / Vedder)

Act III – Defiance

Balcony fills with shouting, ACT-UP demonstrators encircling overhead.

ACT UP! FIGHT BACK! FIGHT AIDS!

PEOPLE WITH AIDS ARE UNDER ATTACK! WHAT DO WE DO? ACT UP! FIGHT BACK!

GEORGE BUSH, YOU CAN'T HIDE. WE CHARGE YOU WITH GENOCIDE!

Three TAIKO appear above them and join the cacophony.

One. Full. Minute.

"Blindsided by HIV, decimated by AIDS, obstructed and blocked by a bureaucracy that could neither comprehend nor respond to what was happening, ignored by our government and dismissed as expendable...we had finally had enough.

"After gathering to take care of ourselves and our loved ones, after creating community out of virulent chaos and from that, creating the San Francisco model of care, we looked about us with the realization that our dying by the thousands wasn't dramatic enough to capture the attention of and elicit action from our own governments.

"So, we took to the streets.

"Taking a lesson from our own recent history, we gathered in force to get in the face of our inactive leaders and a general population choosing to look the other way. From die-ins at the Centers for Disease Control and in the streets of cities from New York to San Francisco, to closing rush hour traffic on the Golden Gate Bridge, we got their attention and caused the release of medicines, the focus of resources, the movement of those bureaucracies such that the help our communities needed on myriad fronts began finally to materialize..."

Enter Keith Boykin:

"Sixteen years into this war with no end in sight. The death toll mounts.

"Evolving from bewildered victims to angry and aggressive activists, refusing to simply die and disappear, we became a Voice, a Presence, a Force with which to be reckoned. By the early 90s over eighteen thousand had died in San Francisco alone, yet even our President had yet to utter a word on AIDS. This nation needed awakening, and awaken it, we did.

"Marches, demonstrations at the seats of our governments, die-ins at the Centers for Disease Control and in the streets of our home cities... If our nation won't respond to our perishing, we will force our leaders to pay attention, and to lead. We will make our country pay attention to us, and we will get our medicines released to us.

"And we succeeded.

"We continue to succeed.

"It has now been thirty years since the war started, and over 25 million people have perished. Last year more than three million people died of AIDS. That's three million coffins, three million eulogies, three million families.

"And this war is far from over. Every ten seconds someone on the planet dies of AIDS. More than 8,000 people will die today from this disease. Nearly 1,000 of them will die before we leave this room tonight.

"Many of us here tonight know all too well the toll that AIDS has taken. We have been fighting this war, battle by battle, deep in the trenches, out on the front lines for decades. And many of us are tired. When we go to the AIDS Grove, when we simply remember what we have lost, when we visit the Quilt, we are understandably heartbroken, for we see more than names and patches sewn into a fabric—we see the faces of our friends, lovers, brothers, sisters, parents, and children.

"We have fought the good fight, but we are a weary army in desperate need of comfort and assurance. So as we gather tonight, we have come to a turning point in this conflict. The poet Essex Hemphill tells us that he conquered his sorrow after the loss of a good friend by taking up the cause of his friend. 'When my brother fell, I picked up his weapons,' he said.

"As did Hemphill, so we must pick up the weapons left behind by our sisters and brothers in the struggle. To those who have gone before us, we honor them not by erecting new statues on pedestals, but by finishing the work that they began.

"Our gathering tonight is not only an acknowledgment, a memorial, but this is our call for a rededication. Tonight we commit ourselves not just to the legacy of the dead, but also to the hopes of the living. We pledge to be vigilant in this fight until victory is won.

"As long as 40 million people on this planet are living with AIDS, we cannot give up. As long as five million people are infected with HIV every year, we cannot give up. As long as there is one person living with this virus, we cannot give up. Until there is a cure, there must be a fight.

"Make no mistake about it, the cavalry will not come to save us. But this is not the time to wave the white flag of surrender. This is the time to fight back. You see, we are the cavalry. We are the ones we've been waiting for. This is our moment in history. We are closer to victory than we may realize, and we have come too far to turn back now. So let us move forward!

"We are morally bound to Answer This Call.

"Battle fatigued and war weary, we march on.

"Sometimes beaten but never defeated, we march on.

"Down but not out, we march on.

"In memory of yesterday, we march on.

"With courage for today, we march on.

"With hope for tomorrow, we march on.

"Will you answer…?"

Creative Catalyst

Act IV

Performers are lined up, as at a bus stop, across the front of the stage...

Rick:
WTF! We did it. Can you believe we did it?!? And Congress actually named the Act after him.

Pam:
Rest in peace, Ryan.

Patrick:
Have you seen that cute Latino guy on "Real World," Pedro Zamora? He has HIV.

Josh:
That's amazing that they'd put him on TV.

Cindy:
It's amazing he'd go on TV.

Roger:
I hear the FDA is working on some fast track process for AIDS drugs...maybe we can get meds before we die!

Rick:
They're calling it a "cocktail," some sort of triple combination...

Josh:
Don't fool yourself. It's no party. The drugs feel just as brutal as the disease.

Cindy:
There are no obituaries in the BAR, today. NO OBITUARIES.

Patrick:
Jesus. Pedro Zamora just died.

Pam:
I just read that they're giving AZT to pregnant women with HIV and it seems to be protecting the infants from infection.

Roger:
I didn't even know it was possible to ride your bike from here to LA. They're making it a fundraiser! Hey, let's do it!

Rick:
Are you crazy?!?!

Josh:
Tom Hanks playing gay, with AIDS!? Antonio Banderas is his lover? I don't even know where to start with that...

Cindy:
We've got to do something about the travel ban. It's absurd. This is the United States!

Josh:
I don't know how many more die-ins I have in me... Probably only a thousand or so!

Roger:
It's called "Rent," and it just opened on Broadway.

Rick:
A musical about AIDS!? This I have to see...

Josh:
It won the TONY?!

Cindy:
It's called Pangaea Global AIDS Foundation—we can't ignore what it's doing to the rest of the world!

290

Pam:
The Ryan White Care Act was just reauthorized!

Roger:
PEPFAR. It stands for the President's Emergency Plan for AIDS Relief. It's about time this happened.

Josh:
A single pill. I can't believe I'm still alive to see my entire regimen in a single pill.

Cindy:
It's amazing how receptive the new administration is to our input.

Rick:
You're not kidding. He's already targeting the needle exchange restrictions and the travel ban.

Josh:
Wow. First Magnet and Stonewall became part of the foundation, now STOP AIDS...and opening up in the Castro; very cool.

Roger:
I really feel hopeful, sometimes...Like, I think we're gonna get through this.

Then a sudden, fully-encircling appearance by the San Francisco Gay Men's Chorus in the balcony overhead, singing "Give 'Em Hope," introducing the CEO and Board to the audience. A quick thank-you-for-coming, and the chorus burst into the rousing chorus of "Defying Gravity" from *Wicked*, as the audience cheered and clapped...

Then, it was liquor and dessert 'til ten.

The important thing here is that we captured and kept the attention of a partying audience through adept, intense storytelling.

Rather than compete with mobile devices, we kept the storytelling focused and intense, thus effectively engaging the audience long enough to communicate, then relinquishing our hold on them for long enough to decompress and express, then doing it again.

When the audience again fell to silence as the lights faded for Act IV, I knew we'd done it right.

18

More Case Studies

T he first rule of production is that it is always easier to apologize than to ask permission.

The United Arab Emirates are, essentially, a federation of monarchies. Beloved, benevolent dictators preside over and protect their respective populations who, in turn, deeply respect and revere their sheiks.

This dynamic manifests in experience creation in some subtle and some not-so-subtle ways, each and every one of them unavoidable and simply a part of the process of work in this industry in the UAE.

The predominant effects are:

The most important seat in the house is that of the sheik. The focal point of any show to be attended by a sheik is the seat in which that sheik sits. From that seat everything must be perfect, and the show must be blocked and choreographed with that in mind, guarding against inadvertent disrespect being shown to the monarch. This translates down to the detail of avoiding any moment when the backs of performers would be turned toward the sheik.

This makes for meticulous and oft-times paranoid scrutiny and second guessing, not only during the concept development and creative stages, but all the way through as successive levels of executives, from vendor to client to, finally, government, must vet and approve what is being produced...with the sheik's protocol officers making their assessment at the very last minute—usually the day before the show.

This puts a lot of pressure on every level of the production and company.

At showtime, if the sheik is behind schedule the curtain is held until he arrives and is seated. Should he be ahead of schedule, we need to be ready to go within moments, often with only a 15-minute advance warning. Everything plays off the schedule and position of the sheik. That's just the way it is.

Another more insidious effect of this dynamic is the fear of offense this seems to engender, most especially in Emirati (or any employee) working for the sheik or in the government. There is such a deeply-rooted fear of offending the sheik that people are afraid to venture out on any sort of creative limb.

Original content is virtually anathema at that level of culture. "Creativity" is applied in the context of lighting and staging, perhaps, and most often at the sourcing of already-proven acts to be brought in and gathered or juxtaposed "creatively" and spectacularly. If an act is a hit elsewhere, the cachet is in the importing of the talent rather than in the creation of anything new.

It's tragic, really, to see so much money spent to bring in "the best," while overlooking the power inherent in a well told, originally created story or experience. The style may change, though the story tends to remain within one of a few "acceptable" constructs. This, then, explains why the same story seems to be told over and over in ceremonies and celebrations in this part of the world. It's about the magnitude rather than the possibility of deeper engagement.

Actually, there's the "scary" word: possibility. It is the possibility of disappointing the sheik that seems to keep the powers that be from going out on the proverbial limb. An irony here is that these sheiks are very likely of the most sophisticated, well-traveled, worldly individuals on the planet. Chances are they've been most everywhere and seen most everything and know far more about what is possible than the legions of deciders and protectors that surround them.

This is my opinion, of course; I've never spoken to a sheik. I'd be surprised, though, were there not to be thoughts of, "Oh, this again?" in the minds of these men as the umpteenth iteration of what's come before is presented at yet another ceremony.

But I digress.

So, yes. The dynamics, creativity, and detail of virtually any experience or ceremony in the Emirates can hinge on the perceived whim or desire of the relevant sheik. Ergo, a month before the grand opening ceremony of Yas Waterworld it came to light that the His Highness was no longer available for a nighttime ceremony. It was going to be taking place in daylight.

When a decision such as this comes down, there is no appeal. It is absolutely what it now is. Daytime.

At first, there was a moment of grief for the beautiful opening ceremony that we'd written...

1. Fireworks: gone
2. Flaming poi: gone
3. Flaming torches: gone

4. Giant, glowing pearls in procession: gone
5. Lighting stunt with the full cast: gone
6. Innumerable, wonderful KO nuance: out the window

Then, after that bit of self-indulgence…

New show—coming right up!

This was actually a fantastic opportunity for creativity, and I can say without hesitation that it was the best thing that could have happened for this show. We had to respond nimbly to the change, and what we created was far more suited to our audience and the venue.

In short, it became an "interrupted" ceremony. It began as a formal ceremony on a wide, floating stage before the primary set piece of a beautiful dhow at the end of a specially-built jetty, jutting into the center of the wave pool. The experience rapidly evolved into an invasion of bandits, the theft of the pearl, the kidnapping of our heroine, the rescue of the pearl and the heroine, and ultimate safe placement of the pearl…a placement that sparked a spectacular six-minute bigger-than-Bellagio fountain show from behind the dhow and throughout the wave pool.

It was a huge hit…and there was one big surprise that helped make it so.

The VIP stage was built out over the wave pool, and from that extended the stage and the jetty to the dhow. At the exciting moment of transition, when the bandits attacked, these bandits were staged in hiding places throughout the set, including under the jetty…and under the stage, about five feet from where the sheik would be sitting.

When the fantastic rubber-faced Sam the Bandit leapt from beneath the stage, he was choreographed to leap, turn, face the sheik and shout, "Yaaaarrrrrrggghhh!!!" with hands outstretched. Now, I never actually said to Sam that that was where the sheik would be sitting. I just aimed him toward it.

As this idea had come to me I thought to myself, "...let's just see how far we get with this...," and proceeded through the rehearsals.

Time came to show it to the client execs. They sat in the sheik's seats. Sam leapt and shouted. They laughed. I don't think they put it together. Now, I didn't actually ask if they thought it would be okay for the bandit to growl at the sheik...but there it was, right?

The sheik's protocol officers came to see a final dress rehearsal. Same thing. Again, I didn't actually point out that this blocking might be considered a little unorthodox; I just let them see and approve without extra scrutiny. I mean, if I know sheiks (and I don't), I believed that he would love the surprise. After all, the man's human, right?

Right?

So. Sheik shows up. Show begins. Lots of pretty and colorful people populating the stage. Slow music. Procession. Cute little Safia carries the pearl toward the jetty. Suddenly, there's a resounding crescendo and the bandits appear from everywhere.

In one fast move Sam leaps up and leans, leering, toward the sheik, arms outstretched and loudly roaring, "Yaaaaaarrrrrrggggghhhh!"

Creative Catalyst

His Highness, startled, looks at him for the briefest of moments, then bursts out in a big, unrestrained laugh. BIG laugh. (I'll bet that no one has said, literally, "Boo!" to the gentleman since he was a child.) He loved it, and continued to chuckle through the rest of the show.

Seeing this, the rest of the cast responded with extra-adrenaline-enhanced performances and the show was a fantastic hit.

Happy client, happy sheik, and I'm quite happy to not find myself in a police escort to the airport.

I believe there is great opportunity for the creative production entrepreneur who is willing to hold the line on creating the best experience possible. Determined to run a production with a strict set of deadlines (and tangible ramifications for missing same), ample time for creative, and committed to raising the bar of compelling connectivity within experiences produced in the UAE and that part of the world. That will include enlightening clients to the rewards of original content and the offering of the strategically unexpected. It will be an uphill effort; I believe it can very likely be profoundly rewarding for all concerned.

POSTMORTEM: A few hours later, after sending all the players back to homes and hotels, the producer and I were in his car, driving back to Dubai. I said, "You know, Adam, I…" and got about that far before he interrupted me with, "Oh, I saw what you were doing and just hoped you wouldn't officially say anything to me about it. I loved it. As long as I could claim ignorance, I figured I'd just stand by to race you to the airport if everything went pear-shaped…"

And that, my friends…

Missed opportunities in Glasgow

Those interested in creating spectacle to engage and move crowds would be well-advised to study the 2014 Commonwealth Games opening ceremonies in Glasgow.

Not, however, as exemplary concept execution.

Unfortunately, it serves as an egregious example of missed opportunities, dropped balls, and what would seem to be poorly thought-through approaches to storytelling and pageantry. At the outset, it must be acknowledged that the simple presentation of the athletes is a powerful and moving component of such ceremony in and of itself. Beyond that, these ceremonies had moments here and there and momentary tableaux of beauty and near-compelling breadth. These moments, though, were few and far between. I believe the producers and creatives responsible for this ceremony let their audience down significantly, leaving it to them to infuse the experience with more substance than was actually there merely out of inherent excitement from such a momentous and patriotic event.

Having more than three years to plan this spectacle, it seems it might have been done so much better...without spending an extra dime. What seemed missing was:

1. Thought
2. Creativity
3. Heart
4. Energy
5. A sense of connection with a live audience

6. The focus on the experience in the stadium
7. And, it would seem…rehearsal!

In reverse order…

A powerful and exciting in-stadium experience, well shot, will translate to the remote audience. This ceremony, especially at the outset, leaned heavily on pre-produced and inauthentic media, draining energy from the stadium and giving the audience at home no sense of spectacle.

The point of being in a stadium for an event is to be where the spectacle is happening. Presenting video after video to those physically there disengages them or, at best, doesn't engage them as fully or as personally.

In fact, throughout the ceremony it seemed that most of the money had been spent on media, animation, and graphics. Had just a fraction of that been spent on rehearsal halls and staging, it might well have made for an exponentially more compelling experience. The result was a relatively energy-free extravaganza that ultimately failed to fully engage.

Being present in the stadium is the only opportunity for the audience to be immersed in the experience. When the show delivered in the stadium is designed for close-ups to be telecast to the remote audience, as was a basic mistake of Danny Boyle's London Ceremonies, everyone is shortchanged…especially the people in the seats.

The positives: The flag entrance was very cool. Nicely done. For the most part, the Put Children First live segments were solid (though the on-screen talent could have made an appearance in the stadium at the culmination). The international chorus was pretty fantastic and the musical talent was superb.

Beyond that...

The very first speaker, Ewan McGregor, wasn't even in the stadium and was pre-recorded. That entire set-up would have been far more compelling were he to have been live and present. Throughout his presentation he would introduce other videos. Lifeless. Unexciting.

Despite John Barrowman's efforts to infuse energy into the opening number, that segment was focus-free and scattered, launching the evening with little foundation or gravity. Just a moment of pageantry to settle the audience and create a feeling of anticipation could have made all the difference. Then follow that by something similar to what was attempted as a light-hearted tour of Scotland, its history, culture, and place in the world.

The Scottish Regiment might have been better and more effectively placed right up front, setting the stage with legacy and portent, making a powerful, emotional connection at the very outset without a word being spoken.

Starting the show with one person in the stands is derivative of televised awards shows and dismisses the presence and priority of the live audience. This is fine at the Oscars, which is a televised event with a live audience. That's a different thing than ceremonial spectacle, which is a live event being televised.

Nuance.

So many slow and sloppy walk-ons of principals and performers.

So much ragged choreography. In three years even volunteers can be rehearsed and deliver crisply. (And God bless them all for their visible and infectious enthusiasm, passion, and commitment; many a show of mine has been carried by volunteer talent, onstage and backstage. I deeply appreciate and respect them all.)

The massive field stage pretty much won the battle for attention in the first segments. So much space, so few people on it. With successive segments on that field, the space underscored the sparseness and looked underproduced and undercast.

Further exacerbating this effect was the poor choice of a "wooden" stage. The blandness of that surface offers no contrast with whatever populates the stage; thus what is on stage cannot be effectively articulated with the lighting...a technique that can effectively "hide" the vast empty space(s) and keep audience focus on the points of action. This is especially pertinent to the small groups that were running around the surface.

A contrasting surface would also have greatly enhanced the beauty of the "500 Miles" ballet, giving it more drama. As it was, it just looked naked. What lighting effects there were, were distracting and diffuse.

Alongside the field stage, the vastly underused main stage stretching the entire length of the field, backed by the massively distracting video screen, served to underscore the relative small physical size of the performers as well as their numbers. Rather than supporting the on-stage or on-field performers with these features, the screens and stages effectively fought with and overpowered the live performers...until the addition of iMag on the big screen was finally used with Rod Stewart and others.

Speaking of nuance...

Rod Stewart truly needs no introduction. His voice and presence would have been a most effective and more exciting "introduction." He might have been better used only once, after the procession. Using him twice dilutes both moments.

Back to the field-long screen. This could have been used for far greater effect than to have been filled with all those expensive and often seemingly meaningless graphics. It could have been used interactively, such that the performers and the screen worked in tandem, collaborating for effect far greater than the sum. Rather than compete with the processional with its big, colorful, distracting animations, perhaps successive and kinetic picture-in-picture images that paralleled the athletes proceeding across the field would have kept focus on the athletes and enhanced the intimacy. Using the relatively tiny, up-high screens for iMag pulled attention from the field and the main stage. Not a good call.

The processional was sloppy and slow. 75 minutes for 6500 athletes is too long. This is where that fantastically-long stage down the side of the field could have been put to great use, introducing each team, shoulder to shoulder, and marching them onto the field. We do know from experience that with this "Broadway" technique, over 11,000 athletes can be brought onto the field in procession in about 45 minutes with great sustained excitement, pageantry, and dramatic energy.

Creative Catalyst

Another missed opportunity.

TelePrompTer. Next to and hidden by the onstage monitors? Susan Boyle? Just asking.

Put Children First. Nice segment and undertone with the potential to be very exciting, though the ball was dropped. How great it would have been, as we'd been set up for this big moment throughout the first part of the show, to see the donation numbers rapidly increase as the entire world texted money to UNICEF. Instead it was "everybody do this and on to the next thing" with no follow-through.

The cameras were a little out of control. During key moments of the program, when actually paying attention to the speaker was probably of the most importance (for the Queen, perhaps, and Malaysia...), cameras were roaming the crowds, seeking candids, sparking the athletes to watch for themselves appearing on the iMag screens and wave to them.

This probably would have been a good time to not do that.

The baton. What happened to the baton journey? All that pre-produced footage of the seaplane arriving in Glasgow, the staging of the baton exiting the plane and the ten-second pyro thing as the baton began the final leg of the journey to the stadium...then, nothing until it showed up in the stadium on the main stage. Another incomplete thought, another broken narrative. Why not just save all that video for the introduction of the baton to the stadium and forego what became the throw-away riverside moment? It didn't serve to move the evening forward; rather, it served to break it up with no payoff.

Was there a rehearsal for the opening of the baton? Her Majesty seemed unamused.

To be fair, by the end the stage(s) were full, the audience and athletes happy. In such events, the basic nature of such spectacle generally mitigates many failings of the production. Pride in the athletes, nationalism, and just the exuberance of all that youth can come together to create an evening of fond memories.

My point is that were it more fully thought-through, with consideration for the audience and engaging use of the venue, the experience could have been profoundly more resonant, compelling, and viscerally memorable.

19

**Experience &
Perspectives**

You may have been told that one should not choose a career to make money. Rather one is best served by listening to one's heart and following one's instincts, choosing a pathway of passion and fulfillment...making a difference in the world in a way that speaks to and nurtures oneself.

Do this, I'm sure you've been told, and the money will come.

Don't. You. Believe. It.

While I fully endorse the authenticity and validity of the first part, I'd be very careful of expectation inherent in "...the money will come." That's not necessarily a bad thing, depending on one's definition of "money," and I dare say it applies to pretty much any career choice. If you love the law, be a lawyer; if you love cars, then drive, design, or repair automobiles...do what feeds you, feeds your muse, and keeps you excited and inspired about what you do.

Be aware, though, that there are no guarantees of financial security, job security, or what one might describe as "success"—especially in the realm of entertainment and creation of experience—if such success has a material quality of life attached.

While it is possible to make a lot of money in these fields, the overarching reality is that a few do fantastically well, some do very well, many do comfortably well, most get by, and no small number scrape by from gig to gig with absolutely no security at all. For many, the price of a can of tuna remains relevant for a great deal of their lives.

You'd best absolutely love what you do, as that is from where the fulfillment must flow.

Creative Catalyst

If creating an experience that makes an audience gasp or cheer or cry out or laugh or go so deeply into their heads that the silence becomes palpable, or leap from their seats before they know what they are doing…if all of this fulfills and excites you, then come on down! There is plenty of room for you here.

If, on the other hand, you seek to make big money as a producer, director, creative director, or designer…and that money is important to you…perhaps you ought to look for something else. You'll sweat blood before you make big money in this spectrum of occupations and careers.

I'm not trying to throw cold water on a career choice. Realism is, at the point of entry, a good discipline to exercise before setting oneself up for disappointment. While the perceived gold standard of Walt Disney Imagineering will always (we hope) offer long-term opportunity for hundreds of creatives and producers along with short term projects for hundreds, if not thousands more, that remains, still, just one company.

Outside of Disney and Universal there are hundreds of entities that hire for thousands of jobs of longer and shorter duration, better and poorer compensation, sporadic to regular work—all of which is in support of creating experience to move and inspire people. That world outside of the Big Guys is a panoply of opportunity for the peripatetic, those willing to travel and move from project to project, month to year…

I worked on three shows during a recent sojourn in Dubai. On the first, a huge spectacle for National Day, we had a team of independents from all over the world. The show-caller came straight from the London

Olympics, one of the choreographers came directly from the Eurovision contest, and the production manager came from South Africa, departing for Hong Kong the day after the close of the show. Even one of my stage managers, within two weeks of the show close, was on the production team for the New Year's Eve broadcast from the Burj Khalifa.

These are short gigs, and there are thousands who make a fair living—not a GREAT living—by moving from place to place, creating something where there was nothing, then moving on to the next thing.

On a larger scale there are installations of all sorts taking place all the time, all over the world. Resorts, theme parks, civic installations, museums, and even churches are creating experiences that take months and years to create and build. On one of these teams, you might find yourself in Shanghai or Dubai for sixteen months to a couple of years, then on to Brazil to work on an Olympic ceremony.

For me, this is exciting and fantastic...and it is not secure. At all. Be sure you are in this for the passion.

I recently spoke on a Themed Entertainment Association board member panel before an audience of students at the Savannah College of Art & Design. What struck me most was that the first questions after the presentation were about quality of life in the business—from both male and female students. Questions that had never even occurred to me back in the day(s) of career launch...

What about family? What about travel? Questions that pertained to the personal, the family environment, downtime and regenerative activity. Not overwhelmingly, but notably, these questions shed light on a bit of a new perspective on career and where it fits in one's life.

A friend of mine, the VP of sales for a company in Southern California, recently vented with me about the point of view of her millennial sales staff. She was getting questions about number of hours a day and time off at a level and time frame that would have been unheard-of a decade or two ago. They were asking how much time they would need to put in to meet their goals, "...they just want to know when they can get off work; it's more important for them to spend time with their friends than to meet quota..."

Of what is this a harbinger?

Observing these questions in the context of the larger conversation articulated in trade mag after business blog after panel discussion in numerous iterations of "How to Deal with Millennials," I sense something positive out of this gradual (or perhaps not-so-gradual) tectonic shift in the work culture as millennials come of age. I sense they seem to want fulfillment, they have a passionate and achievable sense of morality and fairness (and equality), and they want to be fulfilled in their professional pursuits...but they want to have energy left over to enjoy what they've done and time left over to enjoy their families and friends.

So, as I write these words of caution to those about to enter the work force, a part of me is aware that making money may not be the priority for millennials as it was for the baby boomers and following generations. I am also not experiencing the sense of entitlement experienced of GenX and GenY—those who wanted it all, seeking a big salary and expecting to be on a first-name basis with the CEO from week one. While some did get that, most did not and they were not happy about it.

Meanwhile, business leaders and writers seemed to keep analyzing the dynamic as though young people coming up were the problem to solve. How to enlighten them to "how it is" so that business can continue to be run "right."

Looking closer, working alongside twenty-somethings on my own production teams as well as teaching Apple workshops, I see a fresh-faced, aspirational population that may have a more profound effect on the American work ethic than many might envision. For the most part, these kids (I say that affectionately and respectfully—even enviously) are happy with less of the material and seem to find more value in personal experience and levels of intimacy. In my experience relatively few are motivated to acquire, rather to enjoy.

This could change the infrastructure of society in a healthy way, perhaps. Rather than feeling pressure to succeed, I sense a desire for the freedom to accomplish. Rather than needing to make a lot of money, there seems a deeper desire to enjoy and be fulfilled by what they do.

This being the case, what it perhaps portends is that our quality of (material) life may in fact diminish as the quality of living increases as a result of this evolved perspective. And that just might be a very good thing.

Creative Catalyst

Somewhere in there is a great future for the world of experience design, of creation of compelling experience. If one is protective of, and a contributor to, the resonant qualities of one's own life, will that person be even better equipped to create powerful and resonant experience for others? Will they be able to conceive of more effective ways of immersive storytelling, of weaving narrative, of new ways to express narrative or story that can engage on deeper levels? I'm thinking maybe so.

I am struck by something else in these new kids...a level of respect for those who have gone before that I have not experienced in a long time. A desire to learn what is or was, combined with a complete absence of fear for sharing their own ideas and approaches that yield some brilliant, collaborative energy, teaching everyone and benefitting all.

Is it a New World? I dunno. It's certainly a new ethic.

...And it is That Moment that keeps me in this business. The thrill of being able to create an experience that takes people so far into their heads that they are no longer conscious of their minds; they aren't thinking— they are feeling and seeing through some deep, personal portal to which I have found the key.

Rarely will you ever be paid what you are worth. The choice is to let go of any such expectation and to embrace what you do realize from it. This work must nourish you, then. While the money may not come rolling in, you may find peace with the compensation you do receive and find yourself wealthy for having touched others.

Elders, take note

To those currently at the top of their game.

Wanna stay there?

We've talked about the new kids appreciating how much experience yet remains after graduation in order to season them into the amazing creative and technical resources they are going to be. We've addressed the danger to our industries in bestowing lofty titles to the inexperienced and the damage that represents to our quality of product as well as to the crimps and obstacles it puts into the developmental pathways of NextGen.

So, part three of this set is for us old folks, those who've been around and working for a while and aren't in any way ready to leave...and who may feel just a tad threatened by the whippersnapper brigade. All those irritating bright eyes and fresh unwrinkled skin and the ability to pick up any digital device and just freaking use it...

Except, they're not know-it-alls. More to the point, they're want-to-know-it-alls.

By way of illustration, here's a personal anecdote of a key and pivotal moment in my own professional life that enlightened me to the fact that ageism can just as often be in the mind of the older as that of the younger.

As I shared before, after the crash of '08 and returning to NYC in '09, being in survival mode I ended up as a Specialist at Apple SoHo. Entering the store on my first evening, which happened to be an all-store meeting, my already low spirits plummeted. I was clearly the oldest person in the place by at least a factor of two, and for the most part very nearly three.

So, it had come to this. A grey-haired old guy amongst this ocean of youth. At that moment I felt that I may as well have become a Walmart greeter, I felt so immediately irrelevant.

But. I. Was. Wrong.

Grey is just another hair color, and the dynamic on the floor was one of collaborative, organic, supportive teamwork, playing to everyone's strengths and interests. The level of curiosity emanating from pretty much everyone in the place as to what others were bringing to the table was a powerful force, giving me the opportunity to call forth and apply my own tenets of experience creation in the creation of my own experience at Apple...and everywhere.

The most salient of the five being Exploration of Assumption.

I'd assumed a lot about how I'd fit.

What I learned was how curious and willing to explore, how intrigued and hungry to learn were all these nimble minds with which I was now surrounded. How could anyone not be open to learning, with the disparate minds in collective?

The population consisted of everyone from the Ohio frat boy to the Arizona cheerleader, the blue-haired dancer from Denver to the tough-ass dyke from Brooklyn, the Irish lass from Boston, the nerdy music guy from Houston, the German, the Dutch, the theatre geek, the beauty queen, the singer, the writer, the former nurse, the marine, the never-even-thought-about-the-closet downtown boy, the jock...all on the level playing field of technology.

Historically, I've always tended to pick out YPPs (young people of potential) on my teams and give them more than they might think they can handle, tossing them in with me as a safety net and giving them opportunity to discover what's possible.

I now seek and embrace every opportunity to be around, to teach and enlighten, mentor and guide younger men and women, especially students, because

1. They are so hungry to learn and apply what they know.
2. One cannot help but learn right back!

So, back to our conversation and context:

The new kids and NextGen in our workplaces and on our workforces are a huge opportunity for all concerned. They want to learn from you, from us. At the same time, no one wants to look stupid. This is key.

Remember, on the one hand these YPPs come with a fresh body of knowledge from whatever institution or experience brought them to your company or context. They know a lot...of what they've been taught. They also know they haven't actually done anything yet, haven't put anything in the field. That being said, they don't want to look clueless to you.

So don't let 'em feel clueless.

Allow that these kids (sorry, guys, you're still "kids" to us) actually do know stuff. Offer to show them how you do something, and remember to ask them how they might do it. See what they know, appreciate what they know, share what you know and—lo and behold—more times than not a better approach can evolve from the combination of the two.

The more welcoming we are, the more willing to show curiosity and the less afraid to look stupid the YPPs will be. And that is the portal to developing and mentoring new talent and skill. Fear is what stands in the way of any progress, anywhere: our fear of what the kids might represent with respect to our own futures, their fear of screwing up and blowing their first big shot at doing something.

They don't want your job...not today. They want it some-day (probably sooner than is reasonable, but youth is youth—what are you gonna do?). We don't want them to not enter the workforce, do we? We want them to join the team, and we certainly want them qualified to create things. To create experiences of which we have not yet even conceived as we prepare to depart.

The way I see it, we have an opportunity to impart what we know and have learned through doing the work together, to evolve our own processes and enhance our creativity by partnering in mentorship with YPPs. They, on the other hand, have the opportunity to learn from the best while the best are still around.

As they become executives, these kids will be in posi-tions to hire us all for those wonderful consulting fees we see just beyond the horizon, justifiably inflated by our evolved relevance in an industry that is rapidly evolving in its own right.

(And just a hint in that area: it's probably best not to boast of being technologically challenged or one that shuns social media. If that's the case, perhaps you should just be quiet about it. That's not really seen as an asset anymore and, in case you missed it, these are the guys who'll be hiring us at some point. Disparaging the new world doesn't impress those who are creating it. Best you be able to operate your iPhone without cursing. Know how to create a PDF, be facile with digital conferencing technology, and just get over your fear and frustration with the pace of technology.)

Don't be a troglodyte. Have the digital natives teach you how to work your technology.

So, as we encounter the new, we can embrace, welcome, evolve alongside, and remain relevant far longer in collaborative partnership borne of mentoring.

The suggestion is to let go of any resentment and fear. Embrace the YPPs and allow them the freedom to be themselves with you. Everyone will win.

Perspective: the humility factor

What does luck have to do with our career trajectory?

Plenty.

Luck, timing, and circumstance often have no small amount to do with being in the right place at the right time. So taking advantage of a unique circumstance to showcase (or show off!) one's skill or talent, meeting the right person (when they're in a mood that is receptive to what we are or want to be), or whatever series of fortunate events that has led us to the project on which we now work, the title we may now carry is a valuable habit to embrace.

What's the point of this?

The point is that it does us good to remember that there are a lot of people as smart, as creative, as insightful and empathetic, as thoughtful and intuitive, as assiduous and meticulous as are we...currently pumping gas, feeding chickens, weeding gardens, picking fruit, handling garbage, working in plants and factories or...if you can imagine...being lawyers. (Okay, I'm kidding with that last one.)

Some do these things because they want to, though I'd wager likely not most of them.

We are lucky to be in this particular service industry. (Let's not lose sight of the fact that entertainment is a service industry. If we do our jobs well there should be no distractions and the audience is fully taken care-of.) We craft experiences, tell stories in numerous ways, and take people to places they've only imagined or which they may have thought were lost forever. We ease their minds of daily worries while we have them in our hands.

With that luck comes our concomitant responsibility to embrace humility, to guard us from taking ourselves too seriously and allowing us to think we in some way deserve to be doing what we do. A great deal of this, of being where we are and doing what we love to do, is luck.

How can this humility manifest?

Listen. Listen to every one around, especially when developing an idea. Hear as many ideas and approaches as are available before deciding on a course of action. Sometimes what seems the most ridiculous or mundane of ideas can possess the particular germ that inspires brilliance that might otherwise have been missed.

Listen.

Listen to those in junior positions, listen to those in parallel positions, listen to those in no position to make a suggestion. One never knows from where the next idea will come.

Let go of ego. Rarely, rarely, rarely is one guy's way the only way to accomplish something. It may be the way they do it, but frankly, if that's the way they do it every time, that method or process may well be running the risk of becoming stale and irrelevant.

Don't get stuck in past successes.

Listen to suggestion, take out the virtual toolbox, be sure the tools are polished and ready, then apply them to the project or process in a way that is inspired by the goal, by the audience, by the story, by the other minds at the table. Allow the path to success to change with each journey—that is where discovery lives.

Be willing to start fresh, each time. Of course, what was done before will inform what is next accomplished. Yet we can allow for the possibility that a different way might be the better way. To do so, one must be open to the surrounding sharp and creative minds...all minds, actually.

Creative Catalyst

Ignore titles.

People are not the jobs they hold; they are not their titles.

From the microcosm of the workplace, headquarters, or team, where even the new junior member may possibly be the most realistically innovative (okay, rare, but it could happen) to the broader macro of the guy on the street or the bank teller or the gas station attendant. One never knows what experiences bring others into one's own sphere, so best we keep our eyes and ears open to what can come our way. Never dismiss before fully hearing. Actually, never dismiss—what may not be germane today may germinate and grow into The Idea on the next project.

Humility.

The best idea doesn't have to be the leader's. The leader is responsible for recognizing, embracing, and developing the best idea...without ego. That can only be accomplished without ego. Without assumption.

I recently came across a quote by the inimitable Sir Ken Robinson:

The role of a creative leader is not to have all the ideas. It's to create a culture where everyone can have ideas and feel that they are valued.

And the best way to see that a person feels valued is to show that person that they are listened to and heard. Every idea fuels the next one. It's organic; it's creative physics.

And I'll share a grave danger of one who listens protectively. If one is working with a previously envisioned goal in mind and hanging onto that goal, the listening is then false and the energy in the room and the processes undertaken will reflect that falseness, that inauthenticity.

Being willing to embrace the new does not mean the new will prevail, necessarily. It only means the new will be actively considered. And the practical fact is that everything heard, somehow, ends up as some part of the project or result. Whether nuanced or fully articulated, somehow it often all ends up in there.

Everything changes. Be a part of that. Be open to it. One who has the zen discipline to maintain that approach stands to be seen as far more successfully creative... and will in fact most certainly be more successful in inspiring and managing creativity than most others.

Simply keep in mind how lucky we all are to be doing what we love...and that very likely everyone else on a given team is just as lucky, if not more so.

This alone will serve the process and, ultimately, our audiences, ever so well.

Shrink the office—and travel it

Business Model for a New World

Increased Effectiveness

Newly-Unleashed Creativity

Enhanced Collaboration

We are being presented with an opportunity to radically evolve the way in which we do business, specifically, the methodologies and formats through which we gather, manage, and inspire teams to create and collaborate. So much of how we do things are holdovers from ages before, from Bronze to the pre-digital, and I believe these cumbersome communication methods are about to become exponentially streamlined.

The use of remote communication technology has grown, albeit at a glacial pace, since Disney first put video phones in Tomorrowland. With the world now finally moving beyond the pandemic-induced global pause, I see an opportunity to rethink, deconstruct, and reconfigure how we work (and work together) from a perspective of global community. We can embrace this moment, wipe the board clean, restart and come out the other end with enhanced creative product, smoother-running processes, and stronger communication amongst disparate subgroups.

...And save massive amounts of money on commercial real estate and concrete infrastructure!

Were it up to me...

First, some background.

Long ago (and not so far away), at an early SATE conference in Orlando, I shared the stage with the illustrious and iconic TEA Life Achievement Awardee and visionary producer of spectacle, Yves Pépin. In a one-on-one talk show-type setting, we discussed his creative process and the nature of spectacle. While explaining his approach to concept and development, he shared that his first step is always to go where the show is going to take place.

Even if the site isn't yet developed or the venue not constructed, Yves goes to the location before sunset to sit quietly, to experience the sunset and the night while he "lets the area speak" to him.

In my experience, being on-site before beginning creative concepting and development is crucial to the process. Built or not, there is virtually always something intangible that is communicated and transferred to the inner muses through ambience, noises and sounds, smells and light, and simply being in the place where it's going to happen.

If the facility is built, however, this first visit is even more crucial as, in addition to the inspirational qualities above, the realities of a place can inspire vast and various concepts or action out of simple juxtaposition. The placement of doors, the relationship to adjacent architectural or geological features, the height of the ceilings or domes, or the actual architectural or visible infrastructural features can inspire actions or show elements that may not otherwise materialize.

A concept created after the creators have been to the

Creative Catalyst

site stands a far better chance of being best presented and most wonderfully unique to that site.

Further, having as many team members as possible see the site before the show is written makes the visit highly cost effective with respect to the design, writing, and entire production process of the actual show. If the engineers, set and lighting designers, choreographers, composers, and the rest of the team have seen the performance space beforehand, then they, too, can benefit from that inspiration. At the same time, those responsible for materializing the show will see both obstacles and solutions in the aforementioned architecture and infrastructural features.

This all pays off in shorter timelines, less revision, and stronger collaboration.

The reality, unfortunately, is that in practice all of this is a luxury, as it usually involves travel and gathering the team from several locations.

Gathering the team & remote collaboration

Increasingly, human resources for a given project are gathered from various parts of the world. It is not unusual to have, on one project team, individuals located in Amsterdam, Hyderabad, Los Angeles, San Francisco, St. Louis, Chicago, London, and Dallas (an example from recent experience).

This is accepted and can work quite well with one crucial Achilles' heel: the absence of personal relationships, of personal experiences of each member of the team with the others, can undermine the potential collaborative chemistry of the team, render the relationships stilted or impersonal, and infuse a transactional nature to the give-and-take of the collaboration.

However, if a team has previously worked together or has gathered at the outset of the project for a day or two of download and charrette/ideation, the subsequent remote collaboration will be far smoother and productive since there is familiarity and "pheromonal connection" amongst the team.

In my experience, when I am Directing Creative for a project in the UAE or China, the difference in energy, tone, quality of communication, and time it takes to achieve creative milestones between teams with which I am familiar and teams for whom I am merely a face on a screen is vast. However, once I have physically met the team in person, shaken hands, shared a meal, met their kids, asked and responded to basic questions and become a familiar being, once we've been in a room for hours of exploring possibility, the quality of everything ramps right up.

So. Here's what I am pitching in this new, Zoom-friendly era.

Perhaps gather the team on-site at the very beginning. The agenda for the first meeting, then, is the walkthrough of the venue or location. This is a foundational ideation session to establish individual and team responsibilities, general organization, calendar, and timeline for the project...along with initial concept ideation.

From that moment onward, the quality of the work will be higher, the tone more upbeat and productive. The team will prove more cohesive, happier, more flexible and, frankly, more personally committed to the project.

They will have a sense of team that might otherwise be intangible or nonexistent.

How to pay for this?

SHRINK THE OFFICE. I would offer that "home office" staff can be virtually skeletal. A few executive offices and a large, fully-wired conference room is really pretty much all that is needed. Most everyone else can work remotely—full-time employees, PTAN (part-time as needed), short- and long-term contract professionals, consultants, et cetera.

UNDERWRITE WORK-RELATED EXPENSES FOR REMOTE WORKERS. Cutting back on physical plant and the traditional needs of office space will free up sufficient capital to underwrite the necessary internet connections, devices, printers, and so forth.

For less money. *N'est-ce pas?*

This option looks to significantly lower percentages for overhead while offering stronger support for resources even considering inflation and other cost increases.

We're a gig economy. Let's evolve that.

Life is a pathway of opportunity, challenge, success, failure, love and loss, win and lose, responsibility...and relationships. No one really does anything alone, and I am no exception to that.

The creation of this book has been encouraged and inspired by many. The life experience contained herein is the result of knowledge gained and perspective amassed from decisions made and actions taken that have at times been encouraged and embraced, at others discouraged and ignored (with subsequent prices paid as a result). All were freely offered with love—occasionally with an "I told you so" accompanied with something tougher. The sum total of all this is a colorful, variegated life tapestry built of experiences, mistakes, and successes, not one of which I would relinquish as, ultimately, even the darkest times have served to enlighten me.

My only regrets are those whom I have hurt: some inadvertently, others intentionally, all mistakenly.

Here, I single out a few individuals who have been key figures in my life (and to this book).

So, thank you to...

SUSIE ASPELL of Klamath Falls, Oregon, for years (and by that, I mean YEARS) of loving support and editorial oversight.

JANIE SUE PARKER of Chehalis, Washington, for first enlightening me to the universal value and relevance of my writing.

DIANE OLBERG, my editor in the early '80s, who one day looked me in the eye and shared a Key Secret of the Universe: "You know, Kile, success isn't always found in the boardroom…" giving me permission to pursue my passions…and not firing me.

The late **STEVE SILVER** of Beach Blanket Babylon who recognized the nascent creative within and recruited me into the San Francisco ceremonial milieu, passing the virtual baton to me in 1984 and launching this roller coaster of a career.

JERRY MITCHELL, who showed me that The Director need not know all the answers, but know how best to find them in collaborative creative teams that are treated with and inspired by respect and gratitude.

CHRIS GRAP. Superhero, ally, colleague, early investor, ongoing advocate.

ROBERTA PERRY, who suggested I write a blog, then a book, then charge for everything.

ALEXANDRA MORGAN of San Francisco, for her years of relentless support in insisting that I "…write your book!"

JOYCE MALSBURY SLOAN of Portland, Oregon—the gentle artist with whom I walked the Tyrol in the 70s—who read and reviewed the entire draft without flinching.

ACKNOWLEDGMENTS

Stalwart friend **STACY OSUR** of Lincoln, Massachusetts (and San Francisco before that), for decades of active encouragement and for always giving me unfiltered feedback.

Clients, advisors, mentors, and colleagues who have ventured out onto various adventurous limbs with me, with and from whom many a valuable lesson hath been learned: **CHRISTO HARRISON, MICHAEL GRAZIANO, ALAN HATTON, JAY HOWARTH, JOHN FORD, RICH QUIGLEY, JASON FRIEDMAN, FAMEED KHALIQUE**...

MK HALEY, for her enthusiastic advocacy and for showering me with credibility.

LISA J. DAVIS SCHANELY, for her outpouring of generous enthusiasm and experienced advice right when it was needed.

CHRISTOPHER STAPLETON, for stepping in and stepping up with enthusiasm, encouragement, and affirmation at The Perfect Moment.

JOSHUA CAMARENA, brilliantly talented colleague and friend, for truly breathtaking support. You, Sir...Rock.

...And to **JAXON** for showing up when he did and for sticking around. Without you, this would not have happened. Many things would not have come to be.

ACKNOWLEDGMENTS

Having lived and worked throughout the United States and much of the rest of the world for several decades, 'tis notable that Ozier has managed to stay one step ahead of the law the entire time...

...Well, except for that brief stint in the L.A. County jail.

At his core is an innate ability to connect with others. His empathy and sensitivity to the human condition and his passion for life inspire the creation of experiences that resonate personally with each audience member.

From his first production—presenting the private awe of a moonrise to his sweetheart in a rural Oregon theatre consisting of an empty pasture and a bale of hay—he's seen the world as a jigsaw of interlocking stages and performance spaces, rich with potential.

Born in California and raised in Oregon, he first journeyed through a wide variety of careers: a floating university, on staff at the U.S. Congress, political action committees, U.S. Department of State, and as an

officer on a national presidential campaign. After that he left politics and moved to San Francisco, which led him to a performance in a kick line of New Year's Eve Beefcake Babies in Steve Silver's Beach Blanket Babylon. Then, life became really interesting.

Since then, Ozier has lived and worked in San Francisco, LA, Orlando, NYC, Milan, Melbourne, Dubai...throughout Europe, Asia, the Middle East, and Australia. If it weren't for the term "gig economy" one might think that The Guy just can't hold a job.

His work can inspire people to cheer, weep, gasp—and sometimes write checks—through theatre, show, and ceremony in stadium, theme park, outdoor and indoor civic space, touring and destination theatre...and aircraft carrier.

On Kile's teams it's never just a job. Everyone learns, everyone teaches. Teaching through mentorship—apprenticeship—is his passion. Discovering aptitude and nurturing and releasing potential into the world is what most inspires him.

That being said, he is most proud of his recipe for roast chicken, for being labeled "The Jedi of Hugs," and for surviving his life...so far.

Kile Ozier

kile@kileozier.com
oziercreative.guru
imho.kileozier.com
linkedin.com/in/kileozier
youtube.com/@KileOzier

2261 Market Street - #404a
San Francisco, CA 94114

ABOUT THE AUTHOR

Made in the USA
Las Vegas, NV
22 December 2023

83352587R00193